THE OHIO CANALS

Second Edition

FRANK WILCOX

Selected and edited by William A. McGill
With a New Introduction by Lynn Metzger and Peg Bobel

A pictorial survey of the Ohio canals using the drawings and paintings of Frank Wilcox

supplemented by selections of text by the artist

with revisions by William A. McGill

THE KENT STATE UNIVERSITY PRESS

Kent, Ohio

Preface

As a painter, Frank Wilcox reigned supreme when he set out upon a comprehensive journey into an area that totally captivated his interest and imagination. His efforts, usually sustained over a period of years, gave birth to countless studies and sketches made in the field, dozens of preliminary essays, several full–size color renditions; and finally—with a vast backlog of information and understanding—he then unleashed a spontaneous wet–into–wet watercolor that vibrates with the dynamic force he always conveyed.

This series of paintings, sketches, studies, and drawings treating the early canals in Ohio well exemplifies this process. A lesser artist might have been content to merely insinuate the countless details of locale and costume that are necessary for historical accuracy. Instead Mr. Wilcox walked the tow-paths, sought out the hidden and overgrown vestiges of moss–covered locks, and personally researched every mile of the long–lost major canals in the state. With his gifted brush he captured the nostalgia of the remembered past. This warmth and sympathy he communicated with a verve unequaled by many painters.

Rarely today does one ever confront an artist, who with each masterful brushstroke conveys a sense of meaning and worth to what he does. However, Frank Wilcox was such an artist. Because of his sincerity, thoroughness, and skill, his works make our lives much richer for walking with him by the long untrodden ways.

That which shall be no more, lives on through the dedicated works of one of America's finest watercolorists.

William A. McGill

ACKNOWLEDGMENTS

Frank Wilcox planned the illustrations expressedly for this book but, in the case of the watercolors, agreed to the sale of a few of the originals. To those whose collections include these originals, grateful acknowledgment is made for their kindness in permitting color reproductions to be made for this book.

The following subjects are in the several collections of Mr. and Mrs. Ralph L. Wilson of Canton, Ohio (*Opening Vista*), Mr. and Mrs. Bruce I. Gheen of Shaker Heights, Ohio (*Lock, Ohio and Erie Canal*), Dr. and Mrs. Kenneth D. Bryson of Olmsted Falls, Ohio (*Lock at Maumee* and *Packet at Port Washington*), Baldwin-Wallace College, North Hall, Berea, Ohio (*The Hermit: Ohio Canal*) and The Second National Bank, Warren, Ohio (*Ohio and Erie Canal* and *In the Lock*).

Contents

Foreword

No picture in the pastoral mood could surpass the view of Ohio's old canals in their days. In the 1890's the valleys had regained their verdure after the harsh clearings of the pioneer period. True, the trade on the waterways had lessened, had all but passed away; but this fact only enhanced the restful charm of the landscape. The red bridges, weathered by time, remained; the old taverns still stood; and the locks still spurted water from their mossy gates. What matter if only a few white barges passed in the course of a sleepy afternoon? It was long after they were sighted that their rippling reflections drew near, and there was no reason to hurry at the slow approach of the plodding horses on the towpath.

They have made speedways of the old canals and here and there they have turned the taverns into modern inns; but, even now in places one sees enough to reconstruct the scene as it was when rustling leaves and wind-ruffled water were accompanied by the muffled roar of the sluices and the bubbling of the emptying wickets. The canal boat, the towpath and the horses fitted into the picture; and the wooden bridges and the dripping aqueducts were as much a part of nature as the sod-grown banks and the ancient sycamores.

It has been said that the "Canawlers" were a rough and rowdy set, socially undesirable, but that must have been slander. One likes to think of one last survivor, the picturesque hermit, a muskrat trapper, who so long inhabited the last mouldering barge to rot away in the Pinery Narrows. He at least must have felt the charm of the canal to the last, even if his habitation was of the worst sort for aging bones.

But if this memory is like some old darkened painting,

remember that the picture was once bright and glowing, and quite the fashion. There was a time when the canal and all pertaining to it belonged to an active, earnest, and realistic present. Perhaps to those then living it seemed to be evolving from what was a distasteful wilderness; to our eyes it is a symbol of the ancient, verdant peace of unspoiled nature.

Just as the trails of the aborigine became our highways, so the canal brought roads to the little settlements around the locks; and quarries, ponds, and bridges will long remain as evidence of a colorful culture. The old names of our rivers remain unchanged.

One reading about and studying the various phases of the Ohio and other canals can paint, in imagination, a fascinating series of subjects. These will begin with a wild panorama of river, forest, hill, and prairie and end with the quiet, trim, and pastoral aspects of an agricultural landscape, where settled banks and quiet water reflect the Doric portico and white-painted warehouse or mill where teams and wagons stand and men work in a more leisurely fashion than they do today.

The western woods and grassy prairies were scarcely disturbed when the canal was opened. The trees were taller then than now, and rough fields lined with zigzag fences were like harsh scars upon the hillsides. Many cabins built of logs still stood, but here and there neat white frame buildings had begun to appear at river mouths and crossroads.

First came the tree-fellers and the grubbers and clearers. The foot of the hills along the streams soon teemed with men and boys, horses, carts and barrows, all looking small and ineffectual against the established hold of nature. The forest mould was broken for the first time in many places, and woodsmoke drifted about as brush, stumps, and roots were burned away to expose the line. Men worked with axe and pick, shovel and grubbing hoe to remove the humus of centuries. The dark soil was cast up in two great ridges exposing the yellow clay, the shale and gravel of the advancing ditch. Here were heard the Yankee drawl and the quick retorts of Irish Paddy. The hills echoed with the clop of axes and the clink of picks.

Ahead of the advancing line a few men in linen trousers and cowhide boots surveyed the line with rod, chain, and level and estimated the nature of the work to be done ahead. Behind, at salient points, a close group of workmen dug in the lockpits and pounded down long pilings of oak or elm to reinforce the springy sides. About them were growing piles of stone from nearby cliffs and creek beds, and sacks of water lime and river sand.

We may turn to a springtime landscape when the willows are green and towering hardwoods are still dark and brown. The new earthen banks show ochreous and are dotted with flakes of whitish stone and bluish shale. The winter rains and snows have smoothed them down, and the towpath is, as yet, unlevelled by the passing of teams. The new stonework gleams whitely, and red-painted timbers glow in the neutral landscape. At bridge and lockside people gather to watch the swirling water, as, for the first time, it fills the new-made banks.

It is a warm, sunny day when loud cheers greet the coming

of the first boat to lock through the painted gates. Men crowd on the levers as the new barge bright with bunting passes through. A band plays on the cabin roof, and laughing faces look out from the green-shuttered windows at those who stand along the stonework in gown and sunbonnet or top hat and tailcoat. The lock tender grasps the wicket bar, proud of his new-found skill, and rapturous small boys dance perilously on the stone approaches to the gates.

The change along the waterway is rapid. Hammers and saws make music as mills, warehouses, locks, and slips are built. There is great pride in the almost continuous band of raw new timber that now extends along the way, and the landscape grows ever softer with a farther belt of forest trees as background. Now roads cut through the leafy ways to cross the humpbacked bridges. The swales and swamps of the bottom lands are gone, and rows of corn rise high to hide the banks along the river flats. Upon the passing barges stand mounds of casks and barrels, and the green wales are weathered with lime as they slide past the worn mooring posts.

Now comes a time when gigs and stages wait beside the locks for the coming packet. The deck is colorful with the parasols and gay bonnets of fine ladies, while gallants in the new, strapped trousers warn them of the low-hanging bridge. Chimney-gabled houses are seen on the hillsides, and crowded taverns appear behind the sluice nearby. A hum comes from the grist mill, the tannery, and the cooper shop, and the blacksmith's forge gleams faintly within the door.

Much later we follow down the towpath where the hills grow high and bare, and roofs and masts take the place of wooded ridges. The barges stand there dingily and gape with open doors, while rough men toil about the weighlock. The water now is murky, and a pall of smoke rises above the town around the bend. Sandy, poorly paved roads lead down the hill, where freshets wash the soil across the berme bank. All is business and all is grim, for beside the towpath puffs a loco-motive scornfully passing the silent line of barges. We turn upstream to where the green hills are seen again, and here men are busy digging out a bar which fills the ditch. Here a line of barges waits, and noisy cries are heard within a tawdry tavern. To the west against the darkness of the hillside a long, fast-moving string of lights goes by, but those on the barge give it no heed. We turn and stare upon the rippling water of the river.

Another interval passes. Now the lock is ivy-grown and dim. Dark willows hang above its broken walls and its ditch is empty. Only here and there a pool of water glitters, and down the path the last rain has cut a jagged cleft. The old high bridge is gone, and the new boards rattle across the level as a motorist blinds us with his headlights. In the passing moment he turns a quick curious look upon the ancient masonry and is gone. The night wind rustles the willows and the aspens, and a bullfrog croaks from some hidden pool. The fireflies are flashing in the darkness, and nature, once more, claims the picture as her own.   Frank N. Wilcox

LYNN METZGER AND PEG BOBEL

Introduction to the Second Edition

When *The Ohio Canals,* by Frank Wilcox, was published in 1969, it was already a contribution to the body of literature lamenting the wholesale destruction of historic features of the past. Wilcox, who died in 1964, five years before his book was published, would not have known how much his illustrated narrative influenced a preservation movement and that it joined a multitude of voices protesting the loss of canal history and artifacts. That preservation movement still influences the lives of Ohio citizens today in the form of parks, towpaths turned into biking/hiking trails, demonstration locks, and pleasure boat rides on the replicated canal boats. On the final page of *The Ohio Canals,* Frank Wilcox wishfully notes that some areas would make good parks featuring the old canals. Now much of that wish has come to be. This book should be treasured for its art and stories of the past, but also as a forerunner for saving the vestiges of Ohio's canals for future generations to enjoy.

Although *The Ohio Canals* was published in 1969, Frank Wilcox had prepared the art and much of the narrative materials for the manuscript before his death in 1964. Dr. William A. McGill, a former student of Wilcox at the Cleveland Institute of Art, edited the manuscript for publication. In this book Wilcox provides an interesting and informative story of the canal era. He describes and illustrates scenes of the two major canals and several branch canals in Ohio. Of particular interest to canal buffs of today is his map and list of all the "port" towns along the canals, some of which have nearly disappeared.

When enjoying *The Ohio Canals,* one is struck by the beautiful drawings, paintings, and narrative that express a lingering nostalgia for the canal era. Although it contains wonderful art, the book is also a social commentary on the loss of an important part of the past. Wilcox pays tribute to the role the canals played in opening up the state to commerce and immigrants, and he expresses dismay that communities are destroying the remains of the canals, all in the name of progress.

The illustrations and narrative are clearly the work of an artist who loved the landscape and cultures of the past. It is written with an artist's eye as Wilcox points out the colors, reflections, and moods of the subjects and draws his reader into the past glory of the old transportation system. Although nostalgic, he faithfully chronicles important canal scenes, from the digging of the canal and construction of the locks and boats to the pastoral countryside through which the boats passed. As an artist, he could scrub the scenes of the less attractive aspects of the canal world. Readers can envision the sweat, smells, and noise, thereby enhancing their enjoyment of the art.

As a member of the "Cleveland School" of watercolor artists, Wilcox painted many scenes from his childhood. Both canal lore as well as the remaining structures would have drawn his attention to the canals of Ohio. When he began researching the canals, most of the structures had been either destroyed or covered with vegetation such as wild grapevines. A vegetation-shrouded lock can easily inspire someone like Wilcox to imagine it in the heyday of the canal system. Wilcox not only drew those scenes, but he also researched canal technology of the 1820s and '30s and then sketched scenes of horse-drawn scoops, hand labor, and canal boat construction. Even though he did not witness the scenes he painted, his research probably led him to photographs taken late in the canal era, giving him more of a firsthand view.

His research expressed in both art and narrative helps us to imagine this long-ago world.

This book contains drawings and watercolors that depict all types of scenes, from the making of canals to ice skating on their frozen surfaces in winter. It is alive with passengers on the boats and with people at work digging canals, building boats, and opening locks. "Opening Vista" depicts the passengers on a canal boat as lock gates open for them to proceed. Wilcox's painting details the design of the woman's dress, her skirt billowing, reaching for the hand of a little boy. The boat's crew is holding the poles to guide the boat out, and the lock workers are up top opening the gates; one can almost hear shouts, creaking gates, and lapping water. His drawing of the ill-fated Sandy & Beaver Canal depicts the crew poling through a tunnel. Wilcox was surely aware of the canal lore regarding adventures in that tunnel.

To appreciate his work, the reader has to remember the fate of Ohio canals. In opening the region to the larger world by connecting the state to transportation systems on Lake Erie and the Ohio River, they reduced the isolation of this frontier. Although by the 1850s the state contracted with outside companies for the haphazard maintenance of the canals, it later took back that responsibility. But by the late 1890s, the canals were no longer a viable economic transportation system. The canals always had some disadvantages that contributed to their inefficiency as a transportation system. They required constant maintenance, including filling the muskrat holes in the banks every spring. The canals were frozen for four to five months a year, they were narrow, and at times there were "traffic jams" at the locks. Also the boats were restricted to traveling four miles an hour to reduce bank erosion. But their greatest challenge came from the railroads, which could operate twelve months of the year, were faster, and had routes that were more direct than the canals, which had to follow the watercourses.

After the Civil War, the railroad industry expanded rapidly and, although subject to numerous bankruptcy and economic downturns, it served the heartland well. Although the canals maintained some passenger traffic, they mainly hauled coal, which ironically fed the railroads. Ohio canals were nearly destroyed by the great flood of 1913. What remained were fractured, isolated stretches that were often used as water for industry and for recreational activities in a few small towns. More often, the canal bed was used as a dump or for cradling a sewer line, incorporated into the adjoining field for pasture or crops, or simply covered over. In many areas it was forgotten and abandoned.

Wilcox did not portray the railroads in a positive light, probably because they were part of the reason for the demise of the canals. He is very clear about this throughout the book. He envisions that the stage lines and the canals worked together and occasionally the railroads were useful, but they also were not as interesting or useful to his 1850s story. At the same time, however, he addresses the problems of the canals, such as the need to regulate the water supply and the difficulty of dealing with the topography. For both the Sandy & Beaver and Pennsylvania & Ohio canals, water supply was challenging and the routes and years of operation were determined by water sources and supply consistency. The construction, maintenance, and operation of all the canals involved substantial amounts of political maneuvering and competition among multiple factions.

His narrative also describes the different topography between the often-steep climb of the Ohio & Erie Canal in the northeast with that of the Miami & Erie and Wabash canals in the western part of the state where the terrain was far less rugged. Wilcox notes that the Miami & Erie Canal was built in three sections a few years after the Ohio & Erie and served a different part of the state, relating more to Cincinnati and the Ohio River. The northern part, connecting to the Wabash & Erie Canal, was more oriented to Lake Erie. Additionally, he remarks that the earlier-built Ohio & Erie Canal was in an area with more settlers and fewer Native Americans (since they had been vanquished), whereas the more frontier area traversed by the Miami Canal had larger native populations and fewer European Americans.

Clearly his research was focused and specific, as demonstrated in both art and writings. His wonderfully descriptive narrative includes a discussion on the frontier life, and especially canal life, as a "social leveler," whose wealth or social position could not be distinguished from the everyday folk. "It was a homespun age. Beards and whiskers under the chin make all men look alike, and the dress of women in calico and bonnets might not reveal the subtle difference in any manner indicative of social cast. Besides all this, the intimacy of travel would not have tolerated any behavior denying the more nearly universal democracy of the time." Although his comments are sometimes idealistic, they are supported by earlier narratives of travel on the canal and life on the frontier. There was little time for social distinctions; these came later with economic growth.

Wilcox really loved the canals, and in his research he explored, hiked, and sketched what was left; he went about his research as if solving a mystery. In 1947 he tried to find what was left of the Ohio & Erie Canal in Akron. He notes that he carefully tried to follow the old route and then used his imagination to fill in what was no longer there. He carefully describes the Cascade Locks area that lowered or raised boats through a series of fifteen locks. He even mentions that the squalid tenements, shacks, and garden plots that tumble down the hillside have much to tempt the "etcher's needle and the colorist's brush." He notes that in descending the Cascade the view might not be much different from the canal days. "The locks are hidden in the spreading brush, but the blue hills beyond the confluence can be seen, tempting one to continue on without any haunting specters of the past." Visitors following Wilcox's route today would find that the locks have been uncovered and today's Towpath Trail leads north into Cuyahoga Valley National Park.

In the context of the time, during the late 1950s and early '60s when Wilcox created the manuscript, there were incipient stirrings about preserving cultural artifacts of the past. Wilcox notes that it is natural for the younger generation to want what is new and espouse change. However, he urges a greater appreciation for both the cultural remains and the landscape connected with the old canal. *The Ohio Canals* strives to do just that.

This book is representative of early "voices" that were the genesis of a larger historic preservation movement that resulted in the National Historic Preservation Act of 1966. Wilcox is a leader in lamenting the disappearance of historic landmarks such as remnants of the canals in Ohio. Some of his inspiration may have come from two different earlier efforts. Pearl Nye, who was born on a canal boat near the end of the canal era, wrote hundreds

of ballads capturing the flavor of canal life. These were recorded in the 1930s and later published. In 1954, the old Chesapeake & Ohio Canal and towpath became a focus of preservation when United States Supreme Court Justice William O. Douglas led a group of reporters on a hike from Washington, D.C., to Cumberland, Maryland, in a successful fight against turning that canal corridor into a highway. The 1960s were full of new and ambitious ideas about preservation. The Canal Society of Ohio leader Ted Findley had gathered canal preservation advocates in the late 1950s, and the society was formally chartered in 1961. The society began to publish its small journal, *Towpaths*, in 1963, initiating a campaign to save canal stories, canal lands, and canal-related buildings and structures.

In 1964, the State of Ohio decided to divest itself of canal lands, offering them to local governments. Thus some counties and towns acquired the canal lands in their jurisdictions. A few towns—such as Peninsula, Canal Fulton, and Chillicothe, all on the Ohio & Erie Canal—began restoration efforts and developed tourist attractions. The most hands-on effort to preserve canal history took place between 1967 and 1970, when volunteers in Stark County constructed and launched a replica canal boat, the *St. Helena II*. Preservation momentum in northeastern Ohio grew rapidly, resulting in the creation of the Cuyahoga Valley National Recreation Area (now Cuyahoga Valley National Park) in 1974, preserving twenty miles of historic canal and related buildings and structures. As the National Park Service rebuilt the old towpath into a bike/hike trail, the public began to understand the value of the historic resource, leading eventually to the designation of the Ohio & Erie Canal National Heritage

Corridor (now the Ohio & Erie Canalway) in 1996. Today the heritage area stretches along the historic canal from Cleveland to New Philadelphia, and its Towpath Trail is 90 percent complete. In the western part of the state, the Miami & Erie Canal contains numerous segments of towpath that have been restored as a bike/hike trail with parks along the way.

Although the Sandy & Beaver Canal has received random preservation attention, many features are just there to be discovered, some covered with vegetation, but they have not been dismantled or repurposed. The historic features of the Pennsylvania & Ohio are a struggle to find; most are overgrown and receive little public attention. They remain much as Wilcox described them, hidden in the brambles.

Frank Wilcox's art and narrative helped illustrate the charm of a time gone by. In doing so, it caught the attention of readers sometimes distraught by the rapid social and cultural changes taking place, drawing them to what seemed like a more orderly and somehow more peaceful past. The book's elegant watercolors and pastoral scenes still bring together both beauty and frontier life and remind citizens to cherish what went before. Surely Wilcox would be pleased to fast-forward to 2015 and behold the many miles of restored canal and towpath and acres of parks that have been developed around canal culture and history.

INTRODUCTION

How the Canals Came to be Built

At the dawn of the nineteenth century, the Land Companies painted a glorious picture of the opportunities and advantages awaiting settlers in the western country, particularly just beyond the Alleghenies. It soon became apparent to pioneers that access to markets was lacking, however fertile the soil of the new region. Some of the earlier prospectuses declared that the streams leading to the Lakes and the Ohio River were navigable, but it was soon realized that canals would be necessary before western farmers could market their produce.

At the outset, the idea of railroad had not been established in the minds of practical thinkers, and even when it came, it was thought of as an adjunct to further the effectiveness of a canal system. No one at this time had any conception of the potentialities of the steam road or any idea how soon it would supersede the waterways.

Let us keep in mind the position of the settler west of the mountains, growing corn amid the stumps until the land was cleared for wheat, and with little to sell but timber and potash, corn or raw whiskey. He felt continually the lure of the West, while Lake Erie or the Ohio River seemed to bypass him in the wilderness. He knew of the plan to take a canal west of the Falls in Ontario, and the Erie Canal meant access to the Atlantic and the Ohio River to New Orleans. He had no idea that the Erie was surveyed along an ancient outlet of the Lakes, so that the problem presented by the watershed across the State of Ohio meant little.

However, the outstanding characteristic of Ohio's topography is the main watershed of the state. This extends southwestward from the extreme northeastern corner, only a few

miles from Lake Erie, and follows the lake as far as Doan Brook in Cleveland; then it tends even more to the southwest through southern Cuyahoga and Summit, Medina, Ashland and Richland counties as far as Mt. Gilead. In this region its hilly character gives way to that of a high level or rolling plateau through which flow the Scioto southward and the Sandusky to the north. The hilly land is resumed at the head of the Mad River east of Bellefontaine, but it then becomes a high and level plateau westward through Fort Recovery and over the Indiana state line.

All of the land north of this watershed was once the bed of Lake Erie, and numerous distinct bench levels can be distinguished in this northward slope. The St. Joseph and St. Marys Rivers join at Fort Wayne to form the Maumee which flows northeast by east through a wide level basin formerly known as the Great Black Swamp. This region is now well drained. The Maumee flows in a deep-cut and established channel with no distant hills to be seen throughout its course.

The Sandusky River rises on the high central plateau only a few miles from the source of the Scioto and continues sluggishly northward to the Bay. The Huron, Vermilion, Black and Rocky Rivers all have faster and shorter courses, rising as they do in the high land nearer to the lake. The Cuyahoga does not rise in the center of the watershed, but near its northern edge close to the lake, and flows southwestward until it is obstructed by the great glacial deposits upon the plateau around Akron; this causes it to turn to the lake, cutting a deep valley to its ancient delta now occupied by

central Cleveland. The Chagrin, Grand and Ashtabula Rivers are all compressed into the northern edge of the plateau, finding their way to the lake by more tortuous courses. They do not drain large areas.

It is the great watershed itself which determined the courses of the canals. In only three places is its surface sufficiently flat to permit the formation of natural ponds to serve as feeders for the canals: these are the lakes among the glacial deposits east and south of Akron (Portage Lakes), the area south of Newark, and at the middle of the western boundary of St. Marys. The watershed widens as it extends southwestward so that, from the narrow interval between Ashtabula and Warren on the east, it becomes as broad as the distance between Findlay and Sidney in the west. A great wide saddle devoid of high hills exists at the Sandusky Plains around Upper Sandusky; and here was the shortest portage between the rivers; but, strange to say, there were here no feeder streams or ponds for the building of a canal.

Although the western forest had been well explored during the early 18th century, it was a hundred years or more before any idea of canals in the Ohio region developed. The land was then seen as an almost unbroken forest crossed by long rivers leading into the Ohio and shorter streams leading down from the watershed into Lake Erie. The forest humus made even these lesser streams navigable to small boats. Pamphlets, circulated by optimistic land speculators, painted glowing pictures of the ease by which produce could be marketed from anywhere in Ohio by water.

But as soon as clearings were made and markets were

"Taking on" — animals going aboard.

seriously considered, it was discovered that boats of any real size could not make use of the dwindling watercourses, especially those entering Lake Erie. This excludes, of course, the Maumee, which had long been used as a water highway into the West. To tap the resources of central Ohio, it became necessary to connect Lake Erie to the Ohio River between Pittsburgh and Cincinnati. It was discovered that the favorable nature of the Black River at its mouth did not continue far into the high plateau to the south; there was no extensive ponds there which could sustain a head of water for the necessary locks between that height of land and the lake. On the other hand the lakes, ponds and swamps south of the Akron Summit gave ample promise of a constant head of water sufficient to carry barges over the short portage between the Great Bend of the Cuyahoga and the Tuscarawas Valley.

Before the railroads came, people naturally considered the importance of harbor mouths as well as feeder streams and ponds, so that it is not difficult to understand the quandary of the early engineers. Now that all the ports of Lake Erie are about equally favorable for the transshipment of ore from the Upper Lakes, we must study the terrain of the state carefully to note how wisely the courses of the Ohio and Erie Canal as well as others were chosen.

The higher bench of the greater glacial Lake Erie was overlaid by deposits from the ice movements, making a tortuous pattern of the Grand, Chagrin, and Cuyahoga, as well as creating a series of ponds and swamps among the deposits, which, in the early days, were surrounded by impenetrable timber and which drained mainly into the Cuyahoga system

or that of the Mahoning or the Tuscarawas. But the old Portage Path, well known to Cleveland's surveyors, was also known to be a short but steep route west of these ponds into the valleys of the Tuscarawas and the Muskingum. Such knowledge finally determined the course of the canals.

We have now seen the ground pattern upon which the canals of Ohio were traced. We must imagine them as clinging to the stream beds as much as possible, and then taking the divides where ponds exist or where artifical reservoirs can be made by damming the smaller streams of the high and level areas. Locks are sparse and far apart in the river bottoms, but they cluster thickly at a few steep hillsides or at the end of a long gentle grade.

At Lake Erie and on the Ohio are the larger terminal basins—artifical sheets of water made by embankments or by employing the foothill as a berme bank. Occasionally a canal cuts across the bay of a valley and then there is a wide-water, a place to turn a boat or build a warehouse. The canals were determined by this groundwork of the landscape; little was done that time could not soon eradicate.

We must remember that in the 1820's many of the towns now existing came only by virtue of the canals themselves and it was the terminals and not the intermediate stations which made the routes conform to the topography of the land. Both canals and railroads were forced to respect the gradients, but the flow of water was a very subtle problem when such gradients were unknown. The track required its grading and its ballasting; but, once made, there was no need to watch the upturned earth. However, on the canals, time and again

the careful planning of embankments failed to meet the forces of erosion, and new-cleared lands poured ever-increasing floods to break against the scarcely-settled earth of berme and towpath.

By the time the railroads came, much of this lore of engineering was better understood. The railroad had the benefit of improved implements and power; the canal could not advance itself from an end of steel; the whole system had to be foreseen and built before the first boat could be towed through. The old canals carried rails and ties to build the railroads and so hastened the time when they themselves would prove less profitable.

Along Canal Street – Cleveland.

CHAPTER ONE

Canal Excavation

This chapter does not properly include the surveys leading up to the actual digging of the canals, nor does it concern the legal aspects of the State's claim for land for the purpose. It is written about the actual excavation and how this was modified to suit the nature of the ground it had to follow.

The negotiations of the right of way for the canals did not, in their day, entail the difficulties and legal action met with by railroads and traction lines at a later time. For one thing the canals were frequently dug through public lands which had but recently been taken over from former Indian ownership; and, in many cases, they served to drain bottom land which would otherwise have been useless for cultivation by individual owners. Most of the right of way was freely donated, and loans or donations in money were sometimes made with the expectation of benefits to be derived from the use of the canals. It was in the later days, after the canals had begun to lessen in importance, that many disputes arose. These had to do with land occupied as residential or industrial property, for which there existed no proper title from the state.

The principal feature of the canals was the level, that interval of slack water between locks, for which the upper gate of a lock maintained the level above when not in use. In locking down, the lower gate was closed and the upper opened, so that the upper level was extended to the lower gate, thus permitting the barge to enter and be lowered with the shutting of the upper gate.

These levels seldom differed by more than a few feet, and the number of locks between points varied according to the slope of the adjacent streambed. The so-called summit level was somewhat lower than the natural surface of a divide, being in the form of a cut like that of a railroad, into which the water from reservoirs was deflected to fill the cut and to flow down both ways from the summit. It was often necessary to build dikes and embankments to impound water in swamps which would be too low otherwise, or else would not hold enough water.

Occasionally locks were accompanied by sluices leading surplus water into the adjacent streambed over "tumbles" or spillways. When the canal lay close to a watercourse these tumbles might be set immediately into the bank of the canal, somewhat above a lock. These relieved pressure upon the gates after storms. These sluices or tumbles, sometimes provided with wickets, controlled the rate of flow. In many cases they were set beside the lower lock gates within the same front of masonry, especially when the lower channel was wide. Tumbles were paved to arrest the erosion by the water.

A side-cut was the entrance or exit of a canal upon a stream or lake serving as part of a waterway. In such a case the lower gate served as a guardlock preventing the back-flow of high water outside the cut. A few towns had side-cuts from the main channel, with a guardlock on the canal, so that boats, moored within the side-cut, could not be grounded by a sudden lowering of the level outside.

Early accounts of the building of the Ohio Canal mention the Upper and the Lower Rapids of the Cuyahoga. The Upper Rapids were certainly at Peninsula, but the Lower are hard to determine. The Indian riffle at Southpark is too far from Cleveland to answer the descriptions and the stated distance. The modern condition of the lower river is such that its channel no longer follows the original course. It has been dredged and widened as far as Harvard Avenue which is, by river, close to the point described by the early records. It would serve to indicate the probable location of these lower rapids. Most of the soil north of this line is sandy and forms the ancient delta of the river. There is a long stretch between the Lower and Upper Rapids of the Cuyahoga, and there are comparatively few locks until the aqueduct at Peninsula is reached, where several are employed to raise the level to this aqueduct. Somewhat south of this place the so-called Deep Lock took care of a rather rapid portion of the upper river below the Portage.

One can scarcely assume that the canal climbs the Portage Hill in the path of the aborigine—for he would have taken the hill abruptly without considering the grade for such a short distance. The old canal rose gradually on the west side of the Little Cuyahoga, veering to the west as it approached the line of the present Howard Street. Here it formed the northern edge of the thoroughfare and is recollected by many still living as a picturesque but somewhat unsanitary sight, its waters laden with the refuse of the town and its locks spurting, one directly above the other.

Before they were built, the lines of the canals were usually swampy and overgrown; they were seldom built where the higher timber grew. The river trails of the Indian were usually upon the ridges adjacent to a stream and not along its banks. Therefore, they were of little help in cutting through the forest. We must realize that all streams were choked with drift. Much mention is made in the early records of the amount of grubbing and clearing that had to be done before excavation could be started. These records also indicate that heavy timbers were called for by the contractors, as if these were not ready at hand.

One feature of the canal construction paid deference to agriculture. The fact that many farmers were quite tolerant in their attitude resulted in the engineers of the Miami and Erie Canal postponing their digging until cornfields along the line were harvested. It was a cooperative affair in many cases, the farmers and their hands doing much of the preliminary work and some of the construction under regular supervision.

One of the requirements of canal construction was to cut all trees back twenty feet from the canal proper to avoid windfalls across it. A canal section as awarded for contract varied in length according to the nature of the work required.

The form taken by the channel of the canals varied considerably according to their level and the distance from the feeding watercourse. The Ohio and Erie Canal was carried, for the most part, along a bottom land consisting of clay loam. This was easily dug in spring or fall when it was damp, and it could be tamped into smooth banks. Occasionally the bed had to be cut into shale banks on one side, and sometimes it had to be carried above the general level on both sides. But there was little need of hacking or blasting away rock except in the Black Hand Narrows near Newark. The cross-section of the canal bed and its bermes, or banks, varied according to its position, and the whole system rigidly carried out the rules laid down by the engineers.

12

The so-called feeders were usually large ditches carrying a small head of water into a canal, but in some cases they formed channels of equal volume and could be, or were, used for transport. Such was the Columbus Feeder which departed from Scioto to join the Ohio and Erie at Lockbourne. Some feeders were provided with grilles at the mouth to prevent drift from entering the main channels.

One of the shortest feeders was a mere sluice between the river and the canal just north of the Cuyahoga Portage, where river and canal met at the same level. The Columbus Feeder was a very long channel taking water many miles across a slow descent. That these levels could be determined so well in the early days seems remarkable. On the Miami Canal there was a feeder above Middletown and one from the Mad River near Dayton.

An interesting feature in the reports of the Canal Survey is a description of the methods used in determining the rate of flow in the rivers along which it was planned to dig a canal, or of the streams and pond outlets considered promising as feeders. A temporary dam was thrown across such streams and a gauge set in it measuring the water accumulating per minute. The flow of the Cuyahoga was at that time 4,000 cubic feet.

Often sluices were needed to take care of a surplus of water entering a canal, especially after a storm, and these were constructed in various ways according to circumstances. On the Ohio Canal sluices were used to pass water around locks in the Cuyahoga Valley. Sometimes, as an expedient, the water passed through the culvert gates or wickets of the locks, but these were often choked by drift or left closed or open at the wrong time.

On March 30, 1896, a survey of canal land was made to ascertain the rights of the state regarding land adjacent to the canal bed. Often the basin was carried back to foothills instead of a berme, and after the withdrawal of the water farmers began to till the land formerly submerged. The dimensions of the canals as planned were studied and it was found that they were never uniform throughout. This means that the dimensions of banks were much the same, but the width of the channel varied. The Ohio, Hocking, and Miami and Erie had a minimum width of 26 feet at bottom and 40 feet at the water line. The Wabash and Erie had a minimum bottom of 46 feet and a 60-foot top. The Miami and Erie from Dayton to the Wabash and Erie was 36 to 50 feet.

The original specifications for the construction of the canals are as follows: (1) at least 26 feet wide at the bottom; (2) at least 40 feet wide at the water line; (3) towpath at least 10 feet wide at the top; (4) opposite berme not less than 6 feet.

All banks above natural level were to be 1 foot, 9 inches, for every vertical foot in height. Towpath, nine inches higher on the canal side in all cases when there was not a spoil bank in the rear and when the natural surface was not above the bank. When the spoil bank or natural surface was higher than the towpath or opposite bank, each bank was so constructed as to be at least one foot higher at the face than at the back side. Both banks were at least two feet above top water line after they became solid and well settled, except when the engineer directed the bank to be made low to serve as a waste weir or escape for flood water.

Whenever the natural surface under the center of the bank was at or below the level of the bottom of the canal, the bank was made to remain at least three and one-half feet above the top water line; and when the natural surface of the earth under the center was three feet or more below the bottom of the canal, the bank was raised to remain at least three feet above the top water line after having settled.

A widewater was frequently the result of natural topography rather than a planned basin for the turning of boats or the handling of freight. It was often made by a high canal level backing up some minor stream into its ravine. If this stream could not be included in the level and a spillway placed opposite to take care of its overflow, it was carried under the actual bed of the canal through a culvert. Such a condition often created a fine haven for turning boats, for laying them up for the winter, or for taking on and discharging freight at local points. Widewaters became the origin of settlements or groups of warehouses. These were often right on the water, with hoists so arranged as to lift freight directly from the holds into the lofts. When the shores were shelving, such freight was run ashore on gangplanks. Here could be seen great piles of firewood, staves, shingles, brick and stone. There were several widewaters in the lower Cuyahoga along the east bank, one above Boston, and many others along the Tuscarawas and Muskingum. They also existed in Akron along the "Cascade" where mills were built, and they were artificially dug in other places.

One of the chief engineering difficulties met with in the construction of the canals seems to have been the digging of lockpits. To allow for the use of retaining piling and the thickness of the intended walls, these had to be dug much wider and deeper than the contained water volume. This meant pick-and-shovel work, with the use of much planking and pile driving, which was at that time a matter of sheer muscle power. There were then no power shovels, pumps or rubber hoses to be had. All pumping of water had to be done with simple hand-pumps like those used on the ships of the day. The grubbing out of massive roots and hardpan was a large part of the task.

Occasionally the canal had to be carried over a small stream which passed under it by means of a culvert, but when a considerable river had to be crossed at a high level a wooden or stone aqueduct was built which maintained the level of the canal proper and its supports had to be very strong. Owing to the peculiar nature of the falls and the ravine at Peninsula on the Ohio Canal, the aqueduct at this place was built upon arches of stone of which there was plenty immediately at hand. Many aqueducts were housed and roofed over; they were built of timber upon stone piers. That at Peninsula was solid stone throughout and required no roof.

Water lime is a commodity frequently mentioned in connection with the canals. This was evidently the lime made by burning stone directly on location. The *Scioto Gazette* of September 1, 1825, states that there was a quarry on the line of the canal midway between the Akron Summit and the Cuyahoga and in the middle of the proposed lock stairs of the Cascade. A stream passed across this quarry, making it easy from the nature of the ground to provide the necessary mortar

14

for the locks. Here was also abundant stone for these locks, and it was so easy to get out that four or five men could quarry 75 to 100 perch a day in a condition for use in facing. The problem of maintenance was important.

It would appear that there never was a sufficient force of canal employees on hand to take care of emergencies, such as breaks after freshets or the giving way of the walls of privately owned and privately constructed slips adjacent to the canal. Whenever such an emergency occurred, an appeal was made to contractors by the local Canal Board to bid on the needed repairs, and such repairs had to await the decision of the Board as to the terms of the contract.

Apart from Irish and other imported labor, the digging of the canals was aided by local men and boys. Much of this work could be done at seasons when farm work was naturally slack. A phrase or quotation, probably included in a song of the day, casts a reflection upon the Irish and the "wooden-shoed Dutch." This is evidently a Yankee commentary upon the roistering fighting elements among the laborers along the Erie Canal.

The Akron–Cleveland section of the Ohio and Erie had its "Whisky Lane" in Brecksville township. This road, now called Parkview Drive, led down from a distillery to the river and was freely patronized by the diggers. We can sympathize with them in that ague-infested spot and even favor the original name for its historical significance.

In building the canals, plows were employed along with barrows and carts. Farmers grubbed and cleared the land for four or five dollars an acre in advance of the actual work.

Grubbing and clearing was an important part of the work on early canals.— It was usually done in part by local men and boys.

Timber and heavy planks driven to form wall[...]

Timberwork usually done in lockpits before [being]
invested with stone.

Many locks were built of stone in the vicinity — there at Akron, lay close to a quarry.

Worked stone being set in lock channel.
Power either man or horse through use of
windlasses.

Much backing & filling required
before stone can be set.

ound fitted gatepost

Collar bearing

note niche for gate when open.

mitre sill

pin bearings

floor planking.

Wicket valves variously located in lowest frame of the gate.
Note vertical planking on up side of the gate. Rods lie on this side.

Some gates had shelter on out side of frame for the feet of the
gate operator.

Tow Bridge at Defiance. — Bridge had a smooth rail to guide Towrope — act with an axce if rope
ment took the barge downstream.

A culvert was used to carry small streams under a high level of the canal.

Repairing a Breach with brush and piling.

Although much of the canal route was usually through a valley meadow with double banks either above or below the natural level, it was occasionally necessary to cut into a hillside where washbanks often had to be protected by stonework and bermes had to be strengthened with timber, brush, rubble or pavement.

Owing to the tendency of wash from hillsides to create landslips, the towpath was universally built next to the stream and opposite the hillside; and the channel was frequently filled in with such a landslip in the beginning. It was easier to dig out the channel, however, than to re-establish the outer bank when this occurred. The outer bank was menaced more by the direct erosion of the stream than by anything else, hence the timbering, rubble and brush-work applied to it near the river bank. The whole plan of engineering was more complex than we might imagine.

CHAPTER TWO

Locks and Lock Building

The canal lock with its sluice or spillway usually became the nucleus of a settlement made up of the house of the lock tender, his barns, sheds, and ice house, and, in many cases, a tavern and stables for the horses of travellers. Often a mill stood nearby, increasing the aggregation of structures which otherwise might not have arisen there. There were many such settlements along the canals, usually strung out along the waterway with their haphazard adaptation to the necessities of existence.

When such a settlement became established, new roads were naturally cut through to the place, necessitating bridges. From these a view of the scene was always fascinating. The ensemble had a sylvan tone quite unlike that of a railroad siding which, by its very nature, tends rather to obliterate than to preserve natural beauty. Even the large warehouses, sometimes built in such places, resembled the other buildings in a different scale and never took on the grimy and purely utilitarian character of modern factories and storehouses.

Sometimes the nature of the terrain put the towpath opposite a group of buildings, but when the towpath was on the same side these buildings would be lined up close to it, creating something of the effect of a medieval French village built on its lane. When such a settlement lay next to a wide-water, the more expanded surface increased the pictorial value of the setting and afforded opportunity for attractive arrangements of wharfs and groups of small skiffs and scows, not to mention the pleasing reflections that played upon the quiet water. In many cases the adjacent river gleamed below through its screen of willows, its swifter waters adding to the charm of these quaint and quiet places.

Probably the arrival of a barge or packet created none of that nervous tension always induced later by the warning whistle of a locomotive down the bend, with its accompanying clicking of the rails on the dangerous tracks. No doubt the canal claimed its tragedies in the lives of small children, but in general its shallow depth was no menace to life. There was a degree of danger in the locks themselves, for a full lock held twelve or more feet of water, and carelessness in maneuvering laden barges held its risks. On the other hand the lock, although the most mechanical feature of the canal, held little sign of menace as compared to our modern mechanical contrivances, and travel down the canal at four miles an hour was not like a modern speedway where the subconscious mind is continually alert against possible collisions.

The greatest danger to life and limb in canal life was in working upon the lockpits. They had no efficient means of pumping water or of driving piling, so that there was loss of life from cave-ins and the fall of rocks. The spring of the year was also dreaded, for we hear of bulging lock walls during thaws and of boats being pinched when the water was let out. This was offset, when possible, by the use of timbering and jacks and could hardly have resulted in a complete collapse of the structure.

The very nature of the construction of a lock and the conditions of its environment resulted in an effect upon the eye quite unlike that of any other phase of transport. Its materials were mainly stone and wood. What metal was present did not attract notice; instead, the stonework, dry and ochreous at the top, tapered down into the bronze greens of mossy accretions. Water weeds grew upon the wet stones, and a rich tangle of wild morning glory and woodbine tended to hide the wings or approaches in the summer. There was always a fringe of cattails or arrowroot along the banks, and the turf adjacent to it was usually green from the mists of night. The universal Indian Red of the lock gates and levers took on a harmonious patina from sun and damp, turning into a pale rose in the sunlight and a rich violet in the shadows.

The lock was a partial obstruction to the flow of water down the canal. This water was never completely imprisoned, but spurted in fine streams or sprayed from fissures in the gates. Above the lock clear blue water was seen mainly in the center of the channel, for the obstruction of the lock kept this water somewhat stagnant, most of the head pressure passing out the sluiceway some distance above. Here the sides of the channel would be a brassy green, like felt, and dotted with the yellow heads of cow lilies and the black shadow of their leaves. But for some distance below the lock the frequent opening of the gates left the surface muddy or flecked with foam, and the channel would be washed quite free from obstructing growth. Here, too, the waiting boats would brush the banks and crush the cattails down into the mud.

An especially happy picture was presented when lock and sluice-fall occupied the same breastwork. The traveller coming up would be confronted by this wall of stone, one half a foaming rush of water spreading eddies in the path and the other a red portal from which fine sprays fell. Each locking-through was like the opening of a new page of a picture book:

17

the perspective of things seen before was now perceived from a different level.

Adding to the picturesqueness of the lock at its lower front was the change bridge, its sloping rail polished by the sliding, dripping towline as the mules crossed over. Upon this and upon the tops of the gates, the figures of the lock tender and his helpers stood out conspicuously or became bright spots of color if a leafy background hid the view beyond. The barge, usually painted white with green shutters, became the focal point in such a composition; and, when the gates opened, its twin appeared below it upside down, broken only by the subsiding eddies from the opening gates.

In some cases the bridge of a crossroads served the function of a change bridge. This would be high in the middle to permit the passage of a barge. The steep pitch at either end would slow the pace of passing teams, and drivers would pause when they could to see the entering barge or catch the vista up the waterway. Weatherwise farmers along the canal used it as a sort of record of the seasons. Its impounded water would persist even after the level of the adjacent river had lowered; and, if the canal itself flowed sluggishly, they began to hope that needed rain would come. However, the sluice gates between canal and river were a surer indication of the level of the water. If these were closed and no foamy surface showed, it meant that the canal was low and traffic would be stopped unless the weather changed. But after a heavy storm the local people listened for the roar of dams across the feeder heads, and might even go to see the state of the locks and sluices.

Now that barges or boats of any sort no longer pass through the few remaining locks, one seeing them might well be puzzled as to how it was possible to get a boat through. For one thing there is seldom a place where the water is continuous both above and below. It has often been carried under a modern highway which has superseded an original crossroad, of which the modern bridge is made too low to permit the lock to be used for its original purpose. An example of this is just by the lock at Alexanders on the Cuyahoga. Here the water from the sluice is diverted into the mill, and the water passing through the lock goes out under the highway.

A lock was essentially nothing but a stone-walled channel narrowing down the width of the canal to but little over the width of the standard barges used. It would be better to say that the barges were made to fit the locks. There was a drop of from eight to ten feet between the beds above and below this lock, so that the water level dropped accordingly, leaving a proper depth of about four feet in the channel above and below. The upper gates of the lock held back this four feet of water, and when they were open carried this level down to the lower gates which were closed.

In order to set the barge down to the lower level a step lay immediately under the gates, and these upper gates were necessarily shorter than the lower gates which rose from the lower level and which had no step under them except the "miter sill," against which the lower edges of the gates closed. Usually the walls of the lock were level at the top throughout, notwithstanding the inequality in the height of the gates; but occasionally with a long drop the stonework was stepped down just below the upper gates to the level of those below, and in this case the wooden gates were of approximately the same size.

Both the stone and wooden locks were provided with a timber flooring to insure a level base for the flat-bottomed barges in case the water was let out completely. The canal barges had no strong keel of the type seen in deepwater boats. To guard against the tendency of such a long craft to sag in the middle, the framing of the holds was similar to that used in the aqueducts and bridges, being sometimes counterbraced against downward pressure in the middle. The wales of some barges actually rose slightly midway between stem and stern. The floors of the locks and the approaches to the gates had to be kept free of silt and drift by lock tenders and canal engineers; and in early spring and before the water was let in, a general inspection of the whole system was essential.

There were usually two mooring posts on each side of the lock, somewhat close to the gates but not so close as to interfere with the movement of the great levers. This position brought them abreast of the deadeyes attached to the top of the timbers at the cabin corners. They were heavy oaken posts, well rounded at the top, and the old locks showed deep grooves worn in the lateral stonework, made by the mooring ropes as they slipped during the sinking of the barges in the lock. As this occurred, the rope was payed out from a turn or two around the post. This adjustment of the tension of the ropes prevented the heavy barge from floating against the gates as they went either up or down, for no damage to the mitered edges of the gates could be permitted.

Locks usually spurted water from the seams of the gates and from around the hinge post. It was possible to caulk the panelling, but not the meeting edges of the two gates nor the hinge post in its socket. This post and socket had to fit exactly, and there was undoubtedly much difficulty experienced with new locks until all settling had taken place and final adjustments had been made. The setting of the stones within which the grooves for the hinge post were cut constituted the most subtle part of the construction. There was very little loss of water through a lock in good condition, and when it was not frequently used, the growth of water vegetation and moss sealed up minor crevices effectively.

Below the low-water level of the gates were the wickets and the miter sill. This miter sill and the lower edges of the gate leaves were planed to fit; the angle was of course such as to utilize the pressure of the confined water in tightening the joint. The wickets were built on the principle of a butterfly-valve with mitered panel turning to fit the opening in the gate and were operated by action of a tall, centered rod which extended up to a crank on the wooden main levers. On letting out the water with the wickets, there was a bubbling, surging action of the water below the gates which served as an approach. This was frequently curved outward to reduce the width of the waterway to that of the lock and make it easier for the cumbersome barge to "nose in" between the walls of the lock proper. Here we see the reason for the regulation made in the earliest days that all barges have rounded prows. Sometimes this extra stonework, serving as a breastwork to the corners of the lock, was reduced by steps to the level of the lower towpath, and sometimes it was kept level, especially when a change bridge was to be built upon it.

The main or hinge post of the gate extended upward above the stonework, as did the timber forming the inner edge of the gate, but this did not rise quite as high, so that the great lever beam, about eighteen inches square at its outer end, was higher there and tapered to meet the dimensions of the edge timber. When the gates were closed this lever extended outward almost at a right angle to the length of the lock but allowed for the slight acuteness of angle in the gates. The operator, in opening the gates, thrust his feet against the cleats set in the ground and radiating about the gate hinge. The direction of action in both gates was, of course, identical.

But, before it was possible to open the gates with water pressure above, the wickets were opened to let the water down by degrees while the boatmen adjusted the tension on the mooring ropes; when rising, the ropes were looped over the posts and the tension adjusted by shortening the line, putting the successive subsidiary loops in it over the deadeyes. The wickets were turned by the rods extending downward on the framing of the gate through cleats. Sometimes this rod was merely bent at an angle at the top to form a handle; sometimes it had a crank attached similar to the handbrake on a freight car. The operator of the wicket merely walked out on the top edges of the gates or on a shelf or catwalk built upon the framing on the down side.

The setting of the main gate post and the cutting of the channel for it required the greatest care on the part of the builders. This oak post was fitted with a rounded boss at the

20

bottom to fit into a socket which, in its turn, was set into a heavy block of stone at either end of the miter sill. A half-round depression was cut down through the stone courses of the wall to receive the rounded side of this post, and this channel was also contiguous to a shallow niche to receive the opened gate panel. Above the panel the post was completely rounded to receive the wrought iron collar which held it in place. The ends of this collar were passed through the upturned edges of the anchoring irons and tightened by iron wedges. The anchoring irons were let into the stonework and fastened with bolts. They were curved artistically outward and obliquely upstream.

The framework of the gates, which was covered with vertical planking on the upside, was mortised into the main post as a hinge, and the two wings or leaves met at an angle converging upstream—the two wings setting back by the water pressure upon the mitered sill on the lock flooring. This framing was a simple system of square cells in the bottom course of which one or more were bevelled for the wicket valves.

The construction of the lock entailed more work than might be supposed. In the first place it was necessary to be sure that the walls rested upon a secure foundation, and, when close to streams, it was often difficult to establish solid bases without the use of cofferdams. Since the walls could not be braced on the inside, they had to be thick, and they were often braced by the wings at the ends or by buried buttresses. These wings were often stepped down or up, according to their position above or below the lock, and they either made right angles with it or were built in a quadrant.

The wrought ironwork of locks was of superior quality. It is possible to see some of it today among abandoned wicket rods, pivots and sockets lying among weeds and alluvium. Some of the flattened and shaped pieces which are set into the top of the stonework to hold the collar bearing of the main gateposts did not rust and even promise to outlast the stone. All the woodwork of locks and sluices was painted Indian Red which blended well with the stonework, the white and color-trimmed barges and the background of verdure.

Lock walls were of stone, five feet thick at the bottom, and four feet at the top, with the slope buried on the outside. Buttresses twenty feet long were built opposite the upper gates and seventeen feet long opposite the lower gates; all were nine feet thick at the bottom and four feet thick at the water line. Such buttresses are probably the wings or fronts flanking the gates, especially when the lock was built high above the natural level. But often locks were set deeply, and in this case such buttresses would be perhaps less massive and be buried under the adjacent ground. Weirs and spillways often appear in the lower buttress wall.

The floor of the lock, unless smooth, level rock was found, was composed of solid white oak, hewed square, one foot thick, and laid longitudinally. This base was covered with three-inch white oak or pine laid crosswise. Such lumber had to be free from knots, shakes or rot, well jointed and firmly trunneled or spiked. This flooring was carried throughout the whole chamber. All lock chambers were ninety feet long, fifteen to twenty feet wide and with a lift of ten feet. The so-called wooden locks were partly above ground and had an outside wall of stone with an inner wooden wall, the inside being packed with earth. They were temporary in character.

"Locking through" was the term applied to taking a boat up or down or through a lock by filling or emptying the lock chamber. Ordinarily the lock keeper kept his lock full of water and the upper gates open, for the reason that the "down" boat had the right of way owing to the pressure of the current. When this boat entered and was safely moored, the upper gates were closed and the lower wickets opened. This meant that the mooring lines had to be payed out as the boat settled or the side loops slipped off one by one until the lower level was reached. A heavy boat and a swift current required care in order not to bring the prow against the still-closed lower gates. As a rule four mooring lines were used, one to each post. There was always a tendency for the barge to drift into the lower gates as soon as the wickets were opened, thus putting a strain upon all the ropes at once. If more water passed through one wicket than another, it created a vortex in the lock and caused the barge to swing about and bruise its sides against the stonework. Actually, the boats were built to fit the locks so snugly that the latter difficulty was somewhat obviated. The time required to lock a boat down was about ten minutes.

Sometimes the "change bridge" was built across the stone approaches to the down gate, having a sloping guard rail on the down side rising in the center. On this rail a tow rope could slide as teams passed over to the heel or berme. Such a maneuver took place where a boat waited below on the towpath side and probably where this was narrow. The

21

"down" boat floated out over the sunken line of the other after which the "up" team recrossed to the towpath. Owing to the presence of obstructions, such as the great levers, teams were often unlinked before barges were poled into the lock. With no change bridge an up boat often lay to by the heel bank with its team on the outside of the towpath, the down team thus stepping over the submerged portion. If teams were not unlinked in passing locks, the lines had to be passed by hand over levers, mooring posts and other obstructions.

When a barge or packet floated or was poled out of a lock, the current was frequently so slow that there was no steerage way; this meant that as soon as possible the teams must take up the slack in the towline. If the teams were in tandem, the horse or mule nearest the boat felt its drag first, and this animal was selected and trained to "lean to"—that is, to start the barge moving so that the less intelligent or less diligent animal ahead could be whipped up by the driver. It seems a bit unfair to the first animal that he should also be the one usually ridden by the driver after the barge was set moving.

The towpath of the canals was commonly on the river side bank, so that the rule of the road could not always be kept to the right. Sometimes the "up" boat had the right of way on account of the thrust of the current, and the "down" man slacked up his team and "sank his line" so that the ascending boat could be floated over it. Opposite the towpath was the berme bank, or the spoil bank where a hill had been cut away.

Steersmen dreaded being forced over toward the heel bank, because this part of the channel was often soft and likely to be silted up. Thus it will be seen that the "down" man some-

times had to lay to on this side and lay his line across the bed, in order to permit the "up" man to float over it; and his team was supposed to be halted on the outside edge of the towpath.

The locks on all of the Ohio and other canals became known locally by a name bestowed through association. Some few retained their original number from the point of excavation on the section; others were named from the neighborhood, by a descriptive term, or from some earlier tradition. Many hamlets or towns built along the course of the canal took names of a more synthetic nature, much like the affected names given streets today in new real estate subdivisions. Such names are Clinton, Canal Fulton, Lockbourne, Lockhaven and the like. Even the mere number has a romantic sound today, but what is more suggestive than Lost Lock or Deep Lock? Lock Seventeen was more than a mere lock—it became quite a settlement; and mills built along the spillways often grew to little hamlets like Adams Mills.

CHAPTER THREE

About Canal Boats

There were no racy nautical lines to a canal boat; it usually had a solid, substantial, homely, and efficient appearance. It did not, like so many watercraft of today, stand out artificially and conspicuously in the landscape. All such craft gave an impression of good carpentry, with lines that were the natural result of material and ways and means. Such ornament as appeared was made with handsaws or a good, broad paint brush. The barges were built to carry fifty to eighty tons, drew two to three feet of water, and carried coal, wheat, building stone, and other bulky freight.

The names boldly painted on the sterns had an unaffected and native ring to them—patriotic emblems, party slogans, Indian chiefs, states, the names of far places of the earth, birds, beasts, fish. The packets were patronized mainly by people of wealth; poorer people travelled on the freight barges that also boarded travellers. Many passengers slept on deck or wherever they could. Even the packets seldom made more than four miles an hour. On the barges the fare and proposed speed of travel were "cent and a half a mile and mile and a half an hour."

On the packet boats the best advertised time from Cleveland to Portsmouth was eighty hours; the distance travelled was 309 miles. Fares charged on such packets were usually four cents a mile.

The fore-cabin housed the crew of four to nine men. There was a ladies' cabin aft of this, then the main cabin up to 45 feet long; a bar and kitchen in the stern made up the entire building above the deck line. In the large cabins there were usually three tiers of canvas beds so constructed that they

23

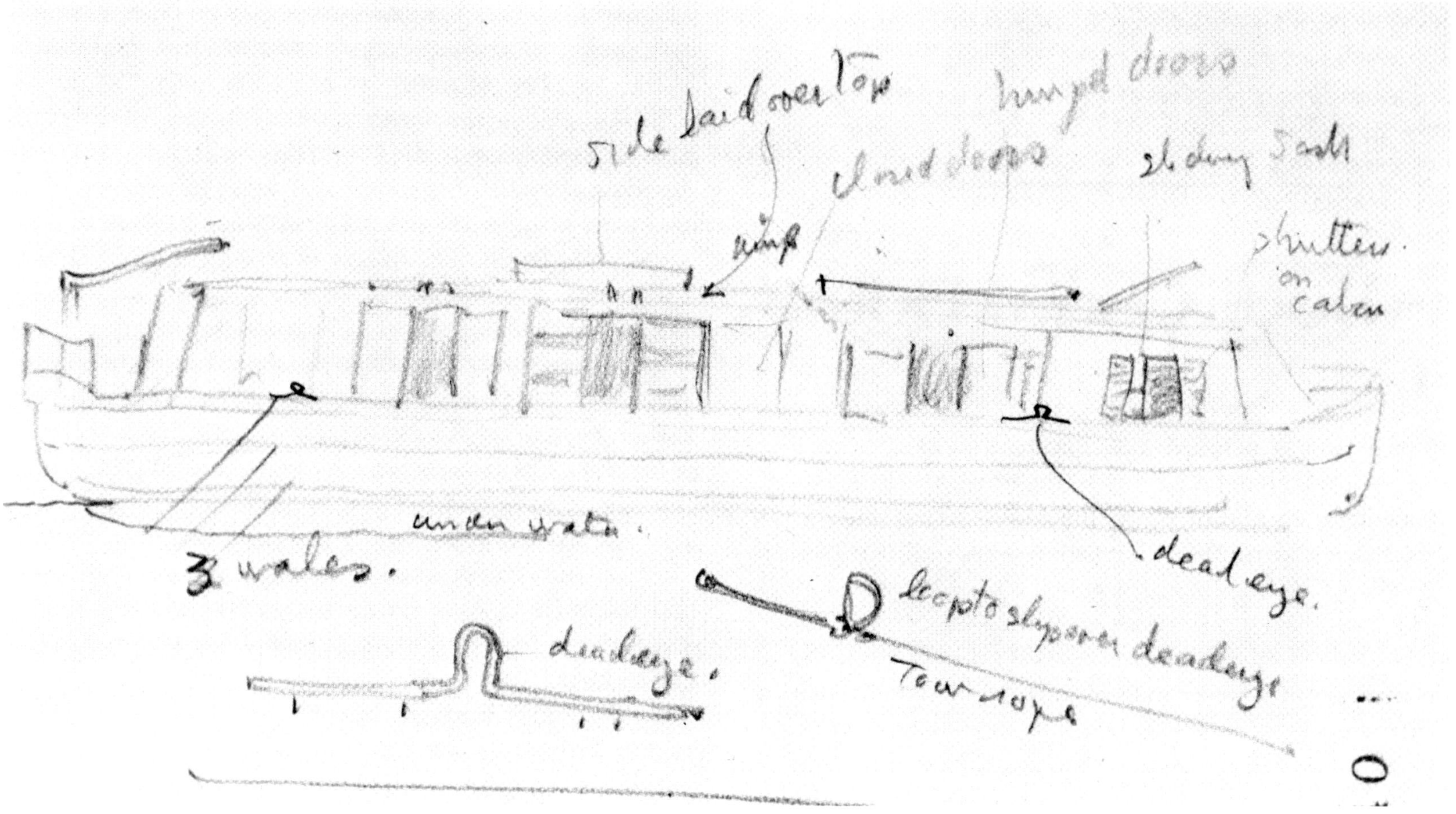

side laid over top   hinged doors

                      laid doors   sliding sash

              wing   shutters
                                             on cabin

under water.

3 wales.

                                          dead eye.

                    dead eye.

                    loop to slip over dead eye

              Tow rope

could be folded away when not in use. They accommodated about 100 people.

The arrangements for living on such a boat would permit only the most democratic behavior, and the close confines of the locks, with the inevitable spectators standing above, would expose all travellers to a minute if not unfriendly scrutiny. Those were the days when nobody expected to be able to ignore others; indeed, travellers were extending a blessing upon isolated people by their passing. In fair weather the passengers gathering upon the decks or roof of a canal boat must have had a pleasant time seeing the mustering of the curious upon the low bridges or about a lock ahead. Many of these would perhaps have produce to sell, or inns or taverns to recommend, or, if nothing more, a question to ask about news up and/or down the canal. It was then a homogeneous and youthful civilization—the kind that Charles Dickens seemed to disparage in his *American Notes*.

The writings of this famous author were not necessarily untruthful. They were undoubtedly an honest expression of the opinions of a clever man of thirty, quite familiar with a wider world, yet perhaps not fully appreciative of what underlay the culture of the America of that day. Only a quarter of a century previous to the opening of the canals, the whole region had been a wilderness, and the sturdy and honest settlers had been much too busy to cultivate the manners of that young English genius.

In many cases canal barges were built by their owners. Such men were often engaged in managing stores, mines, brickyards or other businesses, and also managed their own freighting to points within reach of the canals. Their barges were generally much alike in construction, being merely a squarish hold simply built and braced, carrying cabins fore and aft, with usually a stable amidships. A large tiller was mounted astern and commonly augmented by a great fin suspended by rope or chain to make the rudder effective under slow progression or against a sudden current in which a weighty barge was hard to manage. The fin and rudder could be turned at right angles to shorten the length of the craft in the locks, and the fin could be lifted by the rope. A buffer, usually a curved pipe from the main fore timbers, bent down around the stem and was wound with rope in the middle; this resembled a pair of ox horns. Another smaller buffer was hung by a rope over the stern to protect the rudder post and prevent its striking the angle of the joined gates of the lock.

There was usually a very small raised deck within the semicircular prow where rested the bull's-eye lantern; the tiller deck also was usually higher than the main deck. The prow of the barge was quite blunt and the stem set vertically; the stern was made with an overhang so that a large part of the tiller was below it at all times. When in the lock the tiller was swung athwart the boat to lay completely beneath the stern. The small after-deck behind the galley had a low rail with a gap next to this for easy egress to the lock walls.

Especially characteristic of these barges were the long wales (projecting longitudinal ridges) extending from stem to stern, perfectly horizontal amidships, but rising in graceful curves at stem and stern. These served as buffers against the sides of

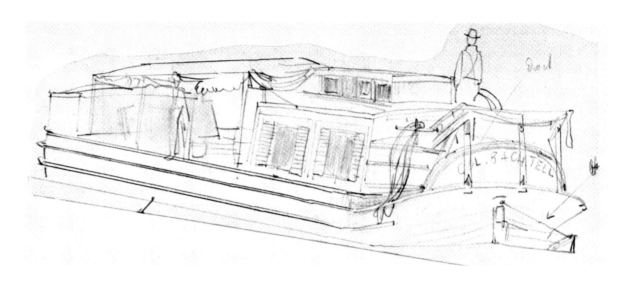

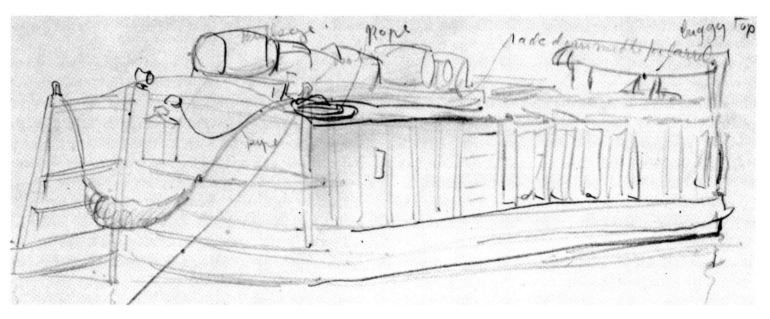

the locks, and also indicated the depth of the lading. The cabin walls, enclosed by the heavy vertical ribs at their corners at the top of which the deadeyes were usually placed, continued the curve of the ribs to the roof, making an effect peculiar to the canal boat. Sometimes a cheaper and simpler construction was used, with straight walls, and in that case the deck housing was continuous from stem to stern.

The side windows were small and fitted with shutter blinds, while the doors to the decks were accompanied by scuttles which slid back upon wooden rails to give head room in descending. Often the deck hatches were made to slide in the same way, and when the deck housing was continuous, there were doors like those of a stable, also accompanied by transverse sliding hatches. On some boats this long roof had longitudinal rails upon which barrels and casks could be easily stowed.

Also on the roofs or decks of the boats were coils of rope for mooring the boat to the four mooring posts of the lock, and also several poles useful in propelling the boat when getting under way or in fending it away from the gates or in warding off obstructions. The skipper's wife often stretched her clothesline from deck house to deck house. Her kitchen chimney stood aft near the tiller on one side. She usually had curtains in her little windows and potted plants here and there. The big, white buggy-top awning that sheltered the helmsman could be folded back upon the rear rail when not wanted.

A boat peculiar to the Miami and Erie system had a housing above the upper wale with sides that slanted inward to a roof that was transversely rounded. It would appear that these boats may not have had a deck throughout. There were double doors almost continuously alongside, and in some cases these had scuttles occupying perhaps a third of the transverse line of the roof. There were combings on these hatches that could be slid back to allow the stowing of large articles. With all the hinged doors removed, the boat would have appeared like a barge with inward-slanting posts supporting the roof. This roof also curved upward slightly in the middle from stem to stern.

Accounts differ as to the location of the stables on freight barges, and doubtless this did vary. In most cases it would appear that the stable was placed amidships, with the stalls built across the keel. The horses or mules walked from the towpath or from the locks over a platform arranged like a drawbridge. Occasionally the stable is mentioned as being forward.

Horses and mules were used to pull canal boats, although all through the history of canals attempts were made to employ steam propulsion. Late in the 19th century a few steam barges came into use on the Miami and Erie Canal to expedite the handling of freight. The space required for an engine and fuel was no deterrent, but horsepower paid better because speed was limited by law to protect the earthen banks from being washed out by the action of moving water. It is probable that the draft animals were selected for strength, endurance, and relatively small size instead of speed, since in most cases they were stabled at relay stations and employed only between two such stations. In this way time was saved with fresh horses and expert handling of the locks.

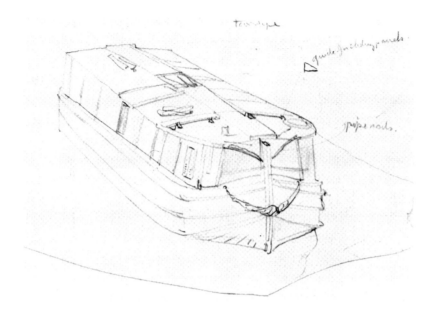

These draft animals were most important. The skipper or captain owned his own animals and saw that they were well provided for in feed, harness, and general care. He often hung a bell on the lead animal and trained the "leaner" or "wheeler" to his duties. This particular mule was hitched nearest to the barge and felt its drag first. He had to be of a proper conscientious temperament to lean his weight on the towline when the driver whipped up the others to take the slack out of the line. The "leaner" also carried the driver when he rode; from that vantage point the driver could nip the other mules with a long blacksnake whip. As a rule this driver was a young man or even a boy of ten, so that his weight probably did not overburden the animal.

Those who understand horses and mules can probably conceive of the problems of managing tow animals under canal boat conditions. It is said that it took a skillful, wary driver to get them aboard or out of their floating stable. On the Miami and Erie Canal the mules wore a peculiar form of blinder, suggesting large, black spectacles at a distance; these were round rather than square and stood out somewhat at the sides.

The harness used in canal boating consisted of a collar, the usual bridle and straps and two tugs attached to a single-tree for each animal. The singletree was attached by a short line or chain to the tow rope with the exception of that of a lead animal which was, of course, hitched to the head of the line. The towpath itself was often narrow and slippery, and these conditions demanded surefooted animals used to travelling tandem like a dog team. Two or three horses or mules were used, depending upon the weight of the barge. The towpath itself may have been on either the right or the left side of the course according to the direction travelled, but it was always between the canal and any nearby river that it paralleled. That this was so is due to the fact that a canal was sometimes excavated from a hillside, and it was entirely natural that the path followed the ridge cast up by the excavation.

In these days of rapid travel over the highways at night, we can imagine slight need for a strong headlight on a canal boat; yet the bull's-eye lantern, burning oil, was hung at the stem of the barge to cast its light ahead on canal and towpath. This lantern was of the old locomotive type and is said to have lighted the way for about two hundred feet ahead—the length of the towline. This illumination made it possible for the snubber to see the banks and the team—though dimly— and for the driver to see any obstruction on the towpath.

The deadeye on the canal boat bears no resemblance to the true nautical object; it was merely a cleat like a short "T" of strap iron bolted to deck or corner post and serving to make fast the towline or the mooring ropes. There was sometimes a succession of loops on the mooring lines which could be placed in sequence over the deadeyes as the rope was payed out or taken in during the sinking or rising of the barge in the lock. The large loop at the end of the mooring line was cast over the mooring posts set on the lock walls. Most pictures of canal boats show many deadeyes bolted down at convenient places—wherever the shape of the boat demanded the fastening of a mooring line. Several lines were needed when the current in the canal was swift.

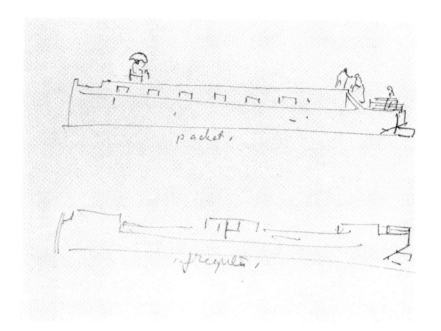

The Hermit: Ohio Canal

Mule Bridge at Defiance

Ohio and Erie Canal

In the Lock

Lock at Maumee

On the Towpath

The Lock Stairs at Akron

River and Canal

Steering the canal boat was sometimes referred to as snubbing. This was not a very active job as a rule, but in avoiding an obstruction under slow way it took considerable muscular power to push the great rudder over with the tiller bar. The helmsman (or woman) usually merely leaned upon the bar in advance of a turn or bend in the canal and the barge responded slowly. A number of long, heavy poles were always lying handy on the deck or cabin roofs to be thrust into the bank, the bottom or the lock sides in an emergency, such as the current's tendency to press the boat too strongly against the lock gates. This was work for an active man or boy, one with sure foot and good judgment as to the right time and place for a good push. Most of the canal barges were too narrow to permit a continuous walk from stem to stern on the same level, so that to "walk the boat" with a pole overside meant quick clambering over the obstructions of freight and deck housings.

The canal boat was so built as to quite fill the standard lock of the canals; and when the lock was full, the barge was well above the level of the stonework. The aqueducts carrying the channel over the rivers were only deep enough to float one barge at a time and just wide enough to let it pass through. This meant there could be no passing of boats in such a place. Peninsula was unique in that a mill stood at the aqueduct and over the roaring falls of the Cuyahoga. The barge passed practically through the mill and then out over the gorge on the high stone bridge.

One peculiarity of the canal barge was the construction of the framing to offset the tendency of the flat keel to sag;

these boats evidently sprang leaks when too heavily laden. One old photograph shows a portable pump leaning in an open doorway of the housing. This pump was obviously made of galvanized sheet iron and consisted of a straight tube with an attached spout and a handle like that of a bicycle pump. It was probably carried from one place to another as needed.

In many places roadways and railways crossed the canal, and lift and swing bridges were built to permit the passage of boats. In the later days it would seem that some railroads scorned even this courtesy to the canal and laid their tracks across without a draw. In such cases a plank would be placed on the towpath, and the mules would enter the stable until the barge had passed under the rails, after which the plank would be reset and they would emerge to renew their task. This meant some heavy labor on the part of the crew to pole the barge under the crossing.

Aside from standard barges there existed canal scows for the transportation of heavy material not requiring protection from the weather. These scows were usually made with rounded corners to save the locks. They were used by the canal operators for the transportation of material for the restoration of locks and banks as well. Such scows were often shorter than canal barges, and would be towed after them with additional draft animals in the team.

There is a beautiful house at Canal Fulton built in the Gothic cottage style of the 1860's. It was quite likely that many canal boats adopted this same general style of sawn plank decorations, because it is probable that many boats

were built by general carpenters rather than by ship builders. There were no special requirements regarding a barge that any sound barn builder or house carpenter could not have mastered; so that to estimate the probable appearance of barges at any particular time we have only to consult parallel house building. We know from advertisements that the interior decoration was quite like that of the inns and taverns of the day, modified by the lines of the boat.

An almost universal feature of barges with a cabin or cabins is the window shutter or double blind. This added much to the quaintness and the domestic appearance of such craft. The degree of intimacy brought about by a boat passing through a lock undoubtedly required this use of shutters. Most cabin windows also had curtains of the ordinary sort behind the glass. Apart from the windows and low-curved roofs the cabins were often beautifully wainscoted with applied planking, and the eaves were sometimes underhung with fretwork. It was no uncommon thing to see potted plants growing on the cabin roofs or on the window sills, wash hanging on a line strung from stem to stern, and the skipper's wife serenely knitting at the tiller bar.

184

sluice

canal

wheel

lock

spillway

183

mill on a Canal

CHAPTER FOUR

The Ohio and Erie Canal

In 1816, Ohio was a great unsettled territory ready for an increased population and a productive industry. It was then that Ethan A. Brown appealed to the Legislature to build an Ohio canal. The state made trial of a lottery to raise funds for such a project, but at length Eleazer Lord of New York interested DeWitt Clinton, governor of that state, who had his eye on the Presidency of the United States. Clinton thereupon approached John Jacob Astor, who loaned the Canal Commission the sum of $1,000,000, taking $600,000 in bonds payable after 1850. This meant high credit for Ohio with bonds selling at a premium.

The size and average depth of the Ohio rivers made an impression upon the public mind at an early date. As early as 1806 the Legislature declared the Mahoning to be navigable as far as Newton Falls, and in 1829 navigable to Warren. Perhaps this change of estimate was due to the increase in size of the barges and keelboats of the day, or perhaps the water level became lower through the cutting off of the forests. In 1807 there was a plan under consideration to deepen the Cuyahoga and the Tuscarawas Rivers—to dredge, clear, and deepen the channels.

As the idea grew, the Cuyahoga and Muskegon Navigation Lottery was organized, with tickets at $5.00 and prizes scaled down from $5,000 to 3,000 prizes at $10.00. The outcome of this enterprise was a plan to build the Ohio and Erie Canal. When the time approached for the opening of this project, the famous Lafayette was on his second visit to America, and it had been planned to bestow upon him the honor of breaking ground; but Governor Clinton of New York took his place.

In the beginning some of the farmers of the region objected to canals for fear that taxes would be prohibitive; but soon after the opening of the Ohio and Erie Canal, they were able to sell their potatoes at forty cents a bushel. After this the canal promoters had little difficulty in arousing enthusiasm for a canal wherever it could be considered an advantage to business. Many routes were discussed and actively planned for which never materialized.

When, on October 23, 1819, a ninety-mile section of the Erie Canal (New York) was opened to navigation, the settlers of Ohio began to visualize greater opportunities for marketing the products of their remote agricultural communities. Ohio people felt that the State of Pennsylvania, with a seaboard of its own, would not attempt to establish a waterway between the Lakes and the Ohio River. Accordingly, a meeting was held at Warren in Trumbull County, in August, 1821, to discuss the desirability of a canal in Ohio. Throughout October and November of 1821 there was continued rejoicing at the near completion of the great canal in New York, and it was seen that immigrants readily accepted invitations to enter the State of Ohio.

In spite of many objectors in the Legislature and among the public, seven Commissioners for Canals were appointed, including Alfred Kelley of Cuyahoga, who was authorized to study the various routes designated, with an appropriation of $6,000. This fact was reported in Cleveland on February 5, 1822. Kelley requested from the public any information relative to the terrain on the watershed—a fact indicating the relatively unknown character of the region at that time.

Later, on April 23, 1822, one James Geddes of Onondaga (New York State) was employed by the State of Ohio to survey the canal routes with a salary for one year of $1,500 and expenses. He arrived in Cleveland on April 25. His work began at Portage or Haines Lake on May 2, and he then left to examine the ground around Ravenna in consideration of a Grand River–Mahoning Canal. This was reported in Cleveland on May 14. He was expected to go to Columbus on May 20 to meet the Council of Commissioners, and also to visit the Killbuck–Black River and the Sandusky–Scioto Summits.

The *Columbus Herald* of May 21, 1822 expressed the belief that the Portage Lake Summit looked very promising, and on May 28 quoted the Commissioners as saying that a Cuyahoga canal would necessitate a lateral channel to benefit the interior of the state. It was probably at this time that immediate thought of the canalization of the lower Muskingum was abandoned, as this river lay too far to the eastward. On August 1, Geddes was still studying the Black River project, and the course of the proposed canal remained problematical.

On August 8 dissension was reported in New York regarding the western termination of the Great Western Section of what came to be the Erie Canal; and on August 22 Commissioner Kelley requested the *Cleveland Herald* to refrain from publishing any news on the Ohio Canal because of the uncertainty of the situation. On September 19, the Commission determined to continue the surveys.

Before winter set in that year, "The Great Western Canal" was completed from Rochester to Little Falls, with daily

35

packets running both ways, and by May 27, 1823, wheat sold fifty per cent higher in New York State. This raised interest in Ohio canals considerably.

As time went on the enthusiasm increased, and on August 14, 1823, an appropriation of $95,600 was raised by the New Yorkers to build a harbor at Black Rock near Buffalo. This fact almost seemed to demand the immediate building of an Ohio Canal. On September 18 Alfred Kelley and Micajah Williams found only about one-half enough water on the Sandusky–Scioto Summit to warrant digging, and so they went again to examine the Cuyahoga–Tuscarawas route and the Killbuck–Black River Summits. Here was the beginning of a heated verbal warfare between the editors of the *Cleveland Herald* and the *Sandusky Clarion*.

The furor over the canal continued to grow. A commission in Washington began to discuss connecting the Potomac with the Ohio, and on February 20, 1824, the Ohio Commission requested an appropriation of $5,000 to complete its own surveys.

It was now considered time to commence surveys at the Cuyahoga Portage, and on June 25, 1825, William H. Price, an engineer from New York, went with Commissioner Kelley to the scene. On August 13, a survey was reported as starting from the Portage to the "Still Water" about four or five miles from Cleveland. This last point was probably about the vicinity of the present Harvard Avenue or somewhat south of it. This survey just about completed the line as extended from the Ohio River to Lake Erie, and the expense began to be estimated.

36

On September 17 Price and James Kilbourne had run their survey to the "Still Water." The summit level was found to be 390 feet above Lake Erie and a few feet below the Portage Pond, thus proving the feasibility of the route. Throughout the rest of the year the public enthusiastically awaited the report of the Commission.

In the summer of 1826 work on the Cuyahoga Section of the Ohio Canal was definitely in progress. The *Sandusky Clarion* was spreading the rumor that there were dire construction difficulties there and that the funds had been used up. Along with this report, the *Scioto Gazette* tells of the problem, on the lower courses, of passing Deer Creek on account of feeders, and whether or not the canal could be completed between Deer Creek and Piketon.

At the same time the line was being located at the Licking Summit and onward to the mouth of the Scioto, at least as far as Piketon. It was decided to employ a high level for the line between Piketon and Portsmouth, since sufficient water was lacking around Chillicothe.

In September, 1826, Commissioner Kelley, because of illness, postponed the letting of contracts between Kendall and Coshocton, but on October 6, he requested a contract to pile rafted square timbers, 10,000 feet, at Cleveland. At the end of the year, it was discovered that valuable coal, then called mineral coal, was made accessible by the canal.

On January 14, 1827, it was announced that the canal would be carried all the way to Cleveland, in spite of short bends close to the easterly side along with drift and sand bars. The added cost was to be $20,000, but this decision certainly altered the history of the city.

In February a rumor spread that certain donations had been made by Clevelanders on a conditional basis, namely, that the canal reach Lake Erie by the east side of the river. It was known that it would cost $6,000 less to bring it down on the west side. This incident recalls the famous Bridge War at Cleveland.

April saw the Commission determined to complete the line from Akron to Cleveland, 36 miles, and Akron to Kendall, 65 miles from Cleveland, by the first of June. On June 22 it was announced that the first boat from Akron was expected on July 4. The distance was 36 miles with 42 locks.

The news of July 6 gives an account of the arrival at Cleveland from the Portage Summit of the first boat, "State of Ohio," all decked with bunting. It bore Governor Trimble from Boston. Ceremonies were held on the Public Square, and a dinner was given at Belden's Tavern. The first freight boat, the "Enterprise" (Captain Guy), arrived on the sixth. It carried flour and whiskey consigned to W.H. Price of Franklin Mills (Kent), through Merwin, Giddings & Co.

The arrival of the first boat in Cleveland marked the beginning of an enterprise which was to last for fifty years. The successful employment of the Cuyahoga Section determined all concerned to complete the Ohio and Erie as soon as possible, and other districts had no desire to lag behind. Work was advanced at points requiring the most careful engineering, and the gaps were filled in rapidly thereafter.

The first reports of the Ohio and Erie Canal survey refer to a place called Kendall, south of the Portage. This name was soon changed to Massillon, for that place was laid out after the building of the canal, and Kendall became the fourth ward of the city. This was in the winter of 1825, after Kendall had existed for ten or twelve years. On January 18, 1826, work on the canal was let out on contract for the stretch between Summit Lake and the second lock south of town, 27 miles of canal.

Part of Massillon's main street is built over the canal, and the lift bridge machinery is said to be still under pavements. The back side of Main Street resembles Venice, and the boiler rooms of the buildings are under the old towpath. Certain lower floors require special insulation against dampness. Here the recollection of the canal must certainly persist. In the early days of the canal so much wheat came from here to Lake Erie that Kendall was known as the Wheat City.

Nearby, the town of Canton, fully aware of the opportunities for expansion presented to Kendall, wanted to build the Nimishillen and Sandy Water Navigation System via Canton, the Nimishillen and the Sandy to the Sandy–Beaver Canal. A great deal of enthusiasm was generated when a plow, drawn by ten yoke of oxen, made a furrow large enough for a small boat to begin this project; but neither this nor the greater project panned out as planned, and many thousands of dollars were lost in the venture (see Chapter 7).

In 1814 a village known as Milan or Mileland was platted on Section 9 west of the Tuscarawas River. After the Ohio Canal was built the settlement of Fulton was established, known today as Canal Fulton. Here it was that Studious Jim, the tow-boy, sat on the bank and read while his barge was loaded with potatoes—he who was to become President Garfield. Canal Fulton grew with the canal, and even now the water from here down furnishes the city of Massillon with power.

The *Advocate* of Newark was a small sheet printed in a quaint, coarse type of 1824. During this year it carried much news about the visit of Lafayette to America, but after January of 1825, changed over to lengthy discussions of proposed canal routes. The Tymochtee Summit for an upper Scioto route by way of Sandusky was considered, also a navigable feeder from Columbus to intersect the main line in the valley of the "Big Belly"—which seems to mean the Walnut. It was stated that there would be only three wash-banks to raise a problem—two on the Scioto and one on the "Big Belly." A feeder over the latter stream would require a dam.

The surveyors were studying the Licking Valley as far as "Tomaka" Creek and a line down the Killbuck from Wooster. It was suggested that Wooster could connect with the Akron Portage through the Chippewa Swamp and, by way of the Walhonding, extend to Coshocton. A line was also run for a feeder from the North and Raccoon forks of the Licking with an aqueduct to carry the former over the latter and so to the Licking Reservoir. It was a problem to construct this reservoir on the Summit. It was to extend eight miles. Here was a marsh enclosing a chain of ponds, with a bank all around except on the northwest near the South Fork a half-mile away. Here the current was reversed in wet weather. The situation required an embankment one and one-half miles

long and six to ten feet high. There was a suitable soil here, consisting of gravel, loam and clay, and there were sufficient streams on the other three sides. There was also Bloody Run Swamp, two miles northwest, which could be included in the system and filled by the South Fork. Quite essential to the success of the undertaking was a deep cut in the ridge, thirty-two feet deep, between the Licking and the Little Walnut.

Five to ten thousand people attended the celebration at Newark when the Ohio and Erie Canal opened. There was a parade to the Summit with salvos of artillery.

Both the lines projected from Newark to the Muskingum united at Wakatomika. The dam eventually built on the Walhonding (White Woman) was discussed at this time. Also included in the plans was the side-cut of Lancaster from the Walnut Summit. This area was to be fed from the Walnut. Here were eventually built the numerous locks which took the Ohio Canal down to the Scioto level.

The Columbus Branch of the Ohio and Erie Canal, or, as it was called, the Columbus Feeder, was begun April 20, 1827. This canal took four years to complete. To make it effective, a dam was thrown across the Scioto at Columbus and various locks constructed, among these the Four Mile Lock. The canal joined the main route at Lockbourne where eight locks were built. The first mile of the Columbus Section was built by convicts from the State Penitentiary, and the first boat through was the "Governor Brown," September 23, 1831. This boat had been launched at Circleville a few days before. On the next day the "Cincinnati" and the "Red

Rover" came via Newark. Soon after this came the "Lady June." All these boats then left for Cleveland, a Columbus band going as far as the Five Mile Lock. At this place the party met the "Chillicothe" and the "George Baker" for the return to Columbus.

The fall of 1829 brought an appeal for a hundred laborers at the Paint Creek aqueduct, and proposals were receivable for forty miles of canal from Deer Creek to the Ohio, with six to eight locks and other works. There were others for two sections at the southern termination of the canal: three locks, heavy embankments, and a forty-foot cut across the isthmus to the Ohio.

The Muskingum Improvement was authorized March 9, 1836, and put under contract October 20, 1836. It conveyed steamboats from Zanesville to Marietta, and a connection from Dresden took canal boats to Zanesville from the Ohio and Erie. This canal had a 154-foot fall, and had larger locks (36 by 180 feet). There were twelve locks in all and a lockage of 125.5 feet.

We see today, in addition to such dams as have been recently built in the gorge above Dover, on the line of the old Ohio and Erie and up the Walhonding Valley, others placed even higher among the headwaters, such as those in the Mohican Forks. It was these streams which poured sudden floods down into the Walhonding and Muskingum and put stress upon the vital line at Roscoe.

By 1838 the following public works were under the supervision of the Canal Commission: The Ohio Canal, Miami Canal, Warren County Extension, Miami Extension, Wabash and Erie Extension, Walhonding and Mohican Canal, Hocking Canal, Muskingum Improvement, and the Western Reserve and Maumee Road and the National Road. It appears that the supervision of the last mentioned roads was a natural part of the forwarding and exchange of freight. The board was involved also in work upon a Muskingum lock and dam below Dresden, the raising of the four-mile level near Cleveland, the New Philadelphia side-cut lock, the Lancaster Lateral Canal, and in making estimates for a Mad River branch of the Miami Canal. There was an examination of Racoon Creek in connection with the Mad River Extension. The navigable feeder of the Miami Canal was being extended, and estimates were being made on the Vernon and Mohican Canals.

On the Ohio Canal, sections 44, 46, 47, and 48 had locks built of stone quarried near Lithopolis, but they were rebuilt with stone from the Hocking Valley. Lock 20 was one mile west of Canal Winchester. The locks west of Winchester (Chaney's Mill) were 19, 20 (Woolen Factory), 21 and 22 (east of Groveport).

Coshocton County included a long stretch of the Ohio and Erie Canal, and the town of Roscoe, opposite the town of Coshocton, was a busy place in canal days. Here the Ohio and Erie had to cross the confluence of the Tuscarawas and the Walhonding which join to form the Muskingum. The nature of the place complicated the problem of carrying the bed of the canal across, and an aqueduct had to be constructed which entailed constant difficulty throughout the history of the route. At one time a waterway was planned up the Walhonding to Mount Vernon and beyond, past many places famous in earlier history and through a beautiful but smaller valley than the Muskingum. Later, when the Walhoning had been abandoned, a three-and-a-half-mile feeder was made of the route by means of a dam across the Walhonding to maintain the level in the Ohio Canal; this feeder lies along the southern side of the valley and runs into the old bed of the canal at Roscoe at approximately a right angle. Doubtless the stress of floods meeting here caused much trouble.

The next letting after Coshocton was Newark. This work was let at fifteen cents per cubic yard. Strangely enough there was a heavy swamp on the Summit where the water flowed both ways after a rain. The cut was three miles long and thirty–four feet at its deepest. This permitted the waters of the "Great Buffalo Swamp" to the east to fill the ditch. Following this the work was carried to Nashport, with a dam at the Narrows of the Black Hand Gorge. There had to be twelve to fifteen locks in this section, as well as two aqueducts and several culverts. Masonry was let at from two to two-and-a-half dollars per perch of sixteen-and-a-half cubic feet. There was great competition here for the work and the stone was at hand.

The next progress was made northeast in Muskingum County up to Roscoe; then work was let at Lancaster for the section down to Circleville on the Scioto. This meant twenty to twenty-five locks, a few culverts and aqueducts, and a dam at Bloomfield. The first six locks south of the Licking Summit were built at a cost of $3.15 per perch, and the facing stone

40

was hauled from Lancaster, eight miles away. At Carroll, Lockport, and Winchester the locks cost $2.50 per perch. There were eight locks just above the junction with the Hocking Canal that were let at $3.25.

The whole course was 309 miles long, exclusive of the 11 miles of the Columbus Lateral and the Dresden Side-Cut and Black Water to Zanesville, which was 17 miles. From Zanesville down, the Muskingum was used by steamboats to Marietta and thence to Pittsburgh. The Muskingum Side-Cut began at Dresden at the mouth of Wakatomika Creek, crossing the river prairies of the Muskingum and leading down to Zanesville where the much wider improvement permitted the ascent of river steam boats from Pittsburgh.

There were long stretches in the canals at a constant level without locks. Sometimes this level accompanied a slow stream, but on occasion the channel was located at a considerable height above the falling creek or river. Normally a drop of ten feet required a lock to equalize the canal and its feeder stream, although a few "lock stairs" existed at the end of a long level. When this occurred, it might be that the higher level was filled by a reservoir or some stream not directly related to that nearest the canal, which was too low or inadequate as a water supply.

The Ohio Canal was maintained by a dam near Circleville for the entire stretch to Portsmouth—the river in this case being below the canal level for many miles. Every summit was characterized by stairs of locks because, on one side or the other, the land fell abruptly, with no adjacent streams of sufficient head to fill all the locks in the series. It was here that reservoirs had to be provided.

Doubtless many who reside in modern Akron do not know that a regular "Cascade" dropped down through the center of the city. Early photographs show us hills sparsely covered with roofs and a few scattered but familiar steeples. These pictures have a bare, austere character, with a wooden, homemade look so typical of that early horse-and-waterpower period. It is rather difficult to determine the earlier ground levels well enough to locate the canal without consulting early maps. That which follows is a list of the locks with the names of streets adjacent, employing the latest maps still showing them:

Lock 1. Foot of the Lower Basin at Exchange Street.
   (There is another in the Upper Basin adjacent.)
Lock 2. Water Street between State and Buchtel Streets
Lock 3. Center Street
Lock 4. East Quarry Street, opposite Church Street
Lock 5. Ash and Bowery Streets, Stone Mill
Lock 6. Mill Street and Canal, Allen Mills
Lock 7. Between Cherry and Howard Streets, Woolen
   Factory
Lock 8. Just south of Market Street
Lock 9. North of Market Street, City Mills
Lock 10. Opposite Tallmadge Street
Lock 11. Foot of Aetna Street, Aetna Mills
Lock 12. Furnace Street
Lock 13. Opposite Spring Street, at B. & O. Railroad
Lock 14. Just south of North Street, Schumacher Mills
Lock 15. Just north of North Street

Lock 16. Foot of Maple Street
Lock 17. Half-mile north of Market Street
Lock 18. Between B. & O. Railroad and Little Cuyahoga
Lock 19. Between B. & O. Railroad and Little Cuyahoga
Lock 20. Just above confluence of the rivers
Lock 21. Just above confluence of the rivers
Lock 22. Just south of Sand Run
Lock 23. Edge of Portage and Northampton townships

The last two locks lie beneath Onondaga George's Lookout, a point mentioned in the reports of Cleaveland's Survey of the Western Reserve.

With the above list in hand, a bright mild day in October, 1947 was selected as the time to explore the old Cascade. This modern survey was perhaps fully as difficult as the original, in that the great masses of modern buildings and survivals from canal days were as troublesome to see through or beyond as a forest of trees. It was Sunday, and Main Street looked fairly empty, and it was quiet at the top near the Goodrich plant. The sun struck almost straight down the thoroughfare, and the strong light made it difficult to define any positive grades suggesting an old canal channel, except that there was a dip in all the streets cutting across Main Street to the north.

Moving down Exchange Street there was no sign of the Lower Basin except that railroad sidings ran through a deep depression and entered the great building of the Goodrich plant; this, according to the list in hand, should be the foot of the Lower Basin. Crossing by Exchange Street, we saw a hidden channel emerging from under the mass of buildings built over much of the old basin, and just south of the street was Lock No. 1 spewing water from its lower gates. The levers, wickets and even the hand-railed catwalks were still intact, and two small boys fished for minnows in the channel. This rustic scene seemed incongruous amid the clutter of industrialism; but there was a Sunday quiet, and irrespressible nature had planted greenery in this cranny among brick walls and cindered lots.

One of the structures hiding the canal in this neighborhood is the parking ground of the big O'Neil department store. This lot occupied the upper shallow valley of the canal Cascade; the depression is deep enough so that the approaches from the rear are fairly steep, and there is also an arching of the floor within the area, indicating the existence of water beneath.

We followed Water Street to the northeast, seeing the channel disappear beneath the foundations of the modern buildings, some of them clearly supported upon piers standing in the rubble-filled channel, which still served as a stream. We missed No. 2 between State and Buchtel Streets. We crossed Center Street and there below to the southeast lay a long lock with an adjacent drydock, intact but for the gates. This may have been No. 3. At this place the canal had already dropped thirty feet from the level followed by the street. This lock was backed by an elevated railroad grade which held it in a green pocket.

More structures appeared to hide the channel again, and Numbers 4 and 5 could not be determined with assurance. It was at this point, Quarry Street, that lock stone was quarried

42

and used to build the locks of the Cascade. The course now taken by the channel was evident in the slope of the hillside and the high angle at which one viewed the roofs below and across the ravine. The new buildings along Main Street and the hills to the east overshadowed the older structures built in canal days. The route passed under a tree-clad height on the left and opposite Mill Street, a suddenly sylvan effect in the midst of brick walls and pavements. Opposite and below was a maze of constructions that hid the site of No. 6 and the Allen Mills. From this point onward there appeared a particularly interesting mass of old buildings of canal and antebellum days. This route took us by way of Cherry Street to West Market Street, and in this maze No. 7 and the Woolen Factory could not be definitely established.

Owing to the importance of modern Market Street, the evidences of the canal and Locks 8 and 9 on either side are not easy to recognize, and, going to the left on Market Street and right on Walnut Street, one comes to a deep, tree-and-root-filled defile that contained Locks 10 and 11; but the Aetna Mills or their successor rises high to the east across a widening ravine. The course is now more northerly as we approach North Street. Just before we reach it, we come to an irregular area marked with evidences of old and modern constructions and also with evidences of nature taking over. This is the site of the Schumacher Mills. Here by a lock with the sluice of old works above it, a Negro lay sound asleep under a tree, lulled by the sound of water in the channel. This was No. 14. Number 15 lay a few rods north of North Street, bearing the date 1907. This was the modern construction in concrete which was little used. We were now on the lower level, having followed Walnut Street downgrade. Here trees, shacks and garden plots are clustered in picturesque confusion on the hillside, and there is yet considerable drop down to the valley of the Little Cuyahoga. Just beyond this point an old sluice disappears into the river, and the next locks, Numbers 16 and 17, are lost in weeds and willows and are probably dry, for the next one on the open bottom land is overgrown with roadside weeds and is easily overlooked. This lock was assumed to be No. 18, and now the journey in this direction ended, as we had reached the point where the main Cuyahoga was visible northward, the bluff of the lower level of North Hill could be seen, and a point at the end of Tallmadge Avenue determined. This is probably the site of Eliakim Crosby's proposed industrial valley, and the end of the avenue is approximately the place where the waters of the Chuckery Race fell over the bluff.

It was now time to go back to Main Street by way of North Street. By walking out upon the North Hill Viaduct, it was possible to see clear up the valley of the Little Cuyahoga to the side of old Middlebury. The route of the Pennsylvania and Cross-Cut Canal could be determined by the depression to the northeast, two miles away; and down below, near the bridge's western end, the afternoon shadows picked out the shallow traces of the race from Old Forge. These traces, however, were interrupted by modern grading for a housing project and were all criss-crossed by railroad tracks.

To follow this old channel through the town is to get the impression that the towering edifices to the east are harsh and garish, and the old mellowed bricks of antiquated warehouses combine with resurgent nature to plead for a little consideration for Old Time's sake. Even the squalid tenements in the lower levels have everything to tempt the etcher's needle and the colorist's brush. At one time the bright red lock gates loosed cascades of white water, and the view up the line was brightened by the painted barges and the freshness of nearby foliage. We may admire the modern in civic architecture; but the canal needed the lower roofs and pointed spires that belonged to Akron in its day. Now it creeps in shame beneath the splendor of a newer age.

When one finally emerges into the open from beneath the overhanging hill west of the Little Cuyahoga, there is to be seen a view which cannot differ much from that of canal days. The locks are hidden in the spreading brush, but the blue hills beyond the confluence can be seen, tempting one to continue on without any haunting spectres of the past. As one descends the Cascade, there is a gradual decrease in the modern and the urban, and an increase in the old yet universally young. The Cascade is, in a way, a symbol of human culture: it represents its rise, its maturity and its decline; it is a neglected monument to the human aspirations which made the modern city what it is.

CHAPTER FIVE

From Cleveland to Portsmouth

Cleveland deserves priority as a canal port in Ohio. Cincinnati, Portsmouth and Toledo, and perhaps Pittsburgh and Zanesville, were hardly unimportant, yet the first section of canal to be operated in connection with all these towns lay between Akron and Cleveland, and Cleveland was the lake port whence the first produce was carried to the Erie Canal and the East.

At an early date there were two cities at the mouth of the Cuyahoga River; Ohio City rivalled Cleveland, and she had done the lion's share in building the lift-bridge at Columbus Street. For a long time the Canal Commissioners debated the advisability of taking the canal over the slack water above the towns and bringing it down the west side of the stream to the old river bed. Had they done so, that natural basin would have been lined with warehouses, and Ohio City would have superseded Cleveland.

But Moses Cleaveland himself had landed at the foot of St. Clair Street, and the sentiments of a generation of the native-born defeated the aspirations of Ohio City. The Public Square was in Cleveland; so was the Court House. What greater argument was needed? People overlooked the fact that the river almost met itself below Vineyard Lane, while every shower washed sand down the steep hillsides. The engineers were aware of this, but the canal needed financial support that Cleveland people were prepared to give.

The natural basin of the canal south of Collision Bend and below Vinegar Hill had its warehouses. The weighlock of the day was down at Seneca Street, being probably the last lift-lock in the series; here undoubtedly was the Weighlock

Building. All the schooner slips were on the east side of the river along River Street, the first being just within the harbor entrance and just north of Lighthouse Street, which led down to the river practically as an extension of Lake Street. Three more slips lay north of the junction of Mandrake Lane, St. Clair Street, and Union Lane. One may still see ancient sail lofts and warehouses of a type then existing. Spring Street led north from Mandrake Lane halfway up the hill under the present site of the Main Street High Level Bridge.

The present grimy Flats were then a picturesque spectacle of tall masts, barges and warehouses interspersed with waters of river and canal. The greenness of the cleared, open spaces was visible. Trees are noticeably missing in the pictures of the earlier period, but stumps often appear in the foregrounds of quaint drawings and engravings in which figures point to objects that were then considered to be of great importance. Apparently these points of interest are the chimney of a new furnace, a new warehouse, a bridge, or a visiting schooner or canal barge.

The term Forest City must have come later than the first engravings. People hated trees until the town grew torrid in summer. The early engravings almost universally show the bluffs well rutted by the wash of showers, and little underbrush appears anywhere. At any rate, one standing on Scranton Heights or by St. Malachi's Church on the West Side could, in 1825, have seen every detail within the scope of that small area. There was little smoke to blot the view. Everyone knew when a schooner was due or when a canal boat was coming down the towpath.

Superior Lane was the center of all activity of river and canal. To the right of it Union Lane ran obliquely down to the original landing where the schooners were tied up. On this street stood Carter's Tavern and all the lodging houses of the water front. Just to the left of Superior Lane was the mouth of the canal, and the basin behind it led across the neck of the loop where, along Division Street, stood all the warehouses of the canal trade.

Spread out fanwise from the basin were streets in the meadow of the loop, with Columbus Street running like a central rib; here were many of the early shops and factories between the East and West Landings. But the true canal emporium was along Canal Street, between Vineyard Lane and Ohio Street; the slips for barges lay west of Bolivar Street. Canal boats did, however, lock down into the river through the basin and guardlock and moored all around the loop and along among the schooner slips of the river. One early map seems to indicate that slips were built later in the low land across the river and through to the old river bed.

Even in the earlier days there was a furnace in the Flats within Collision Bend, this being the eastward point of the second river loop near Ontario Street, and the natural basin lay between. The greater part of this area was, however, a sort of open pasture crossed only by the Elyria Road.

It does not require much imagination to reconstruct the appearance of Cleveland at that time, for the pattern of the streets is simple and the division of industry was clearly marked by the topography. People taking the packets walked down Vineyard Lane and turned west on James Street to the basin or left on Canal Street to the slips below Michigan Street. Perhaps they went down Superior Hill and turned left on Merwin Street, walking only a short distance to the guardlock by the river.

Up Vineyard Lane came all the baggage wheeled in barrows or carried on the shoulders of porters. The better taverns or hotels were to be found from the top of the hill to the Square, and lower Superior Street was the extent of the shopping district in those days. Everything east of the Square consisted of small neat dwellings and gardens enclosed in paling fences; beyond, these gave way to split rails and rough pasture or woodland. It would have been at the west end of Canal Street that hotel runners would have been heard, and Vineyard Lane would have provided a colorful sight when the boats came down the canal.

North, at the foot of St. Clair Street, timid immigrants arriving on lake schooners would have walked up Union Lane, somewhat fearful of the wide and fashionable thoroughfare above. They would have seen bright, new stores and the white pickets around the four green quarters of the Square; between these were the displays of bales and barrels, brought up the hill in carts and wagons. There would have been a fair display of tools, harness and hardware, and the whole street had an atmosphere of the old country store of later days. Lower Superior Street is usually depicted with numerous teams hitched along the wooden sidewalks; awnings shade this walk beneath the quaintly painted tradesmen's signs. The wide, rutted roadway was more than adequate to the needs of business traffic.

Cleveland was founded in 1796 in a complete wilderness. Within a quarter of a century, as contemporary engravings indicate, the town had extended eastward to about East 14 Street, southeastward to a point near Jefferson Street and Broadway, westward to about West 30 Street, and southwest and south to Walworth Run and old University Heights.

Apparently most of the buildings then existing were either frame or brick, for log buildings were no longer represented. Many of the warehouses were four or five stories high, and many dwellings were two-storied. All this building and expansion was based upon lake commerce, and the canal immediately brought about a further increase.

There seems to have been a typical New England neatness to the town. Buildings were painted white with green shutters, picket fences surrounded gardens, and family cows grazed in neighboring lots. A classic white Court House with a cupola stood in the southwest quarter of the Public Square.

The traveller leaving Cleveland by canal found himself gliding southeastward under the high slope of Vinegar Hill; he then passed east and south along the east side of the valley until the Scranton or old University Heights lay to the west. From here onward all was country, and, when the Five Mile Lock was reached, he could see no sign of a nearby town. He may have discerned a road cutting up through the wood to the southward as he passed this lock; this road is now Route 21. Perhaps more people pass along this road today by car than moved along the canal in a year's time. Our traveller would have had at least 90 hours of transit through the green country before he would again see as many people as he had left behind.

Even the gigantic works of our modern age cannot entirely blot out the topographical features which forced the canal builders to dig where they did. If we begin at Lake Erie and follow, for instance, the Ohio and Erie Canal up the Cuyahoga, we will still be able to recognize many of the photographs and drawings preserved for us.

The final lock which let the barges down into the level of the lake was located just south of the foot of Superior Street hill, and from here the canal swung southeastward around the acute loops of the river and along the foot of Vinegar Hill and below the old market district. This took it below old Broadway to Jefferson Street, where it entered a basin and weighlock on ground now occupied by the Great Lakes Towing Company. All of this region was crowded at one time with the slips and warehouses of the canal trade. The canal then continued generally southeastward until it led through a lock just west of the foot of East 71 Street hill at the Willow Cloverleaf. In this stretch the course was close to the eastern side of the flat bottoms. The "runs" entering the valley here passed under the canal through culverts and any overflow passed through spillways.

Beyond Willow with its historic French House and Saguin's Post of early history, the canal led on to Tinkers Creek in the vicinity of the Moravian settlement of Pilgerruh near which the Mahoning Trail from the west side crossed the Cuyahoga in its course to Fort Pitt. The canal continued close to the steep eastern hillsides until it passed the shale cliffs of the Pinery just north of the Brecksville–Northfield bridge. It then passed the end of the Chippewa Hogback and

Duel — Toledo Terminus.

entered the ancient Cuyahoga Lake at Vaughn (Jaite) where a pronounced second bottom is to be seen across the river. Just here stood the old Red Lock by the Little York road.

The valley becomes narrower at Boston where a dam was built in the river, and just before Peninsula is reached the course swung westerly around the promontory and crossed the stony gorge on an aqueduct. At this point, the course of the canal follows the west side of the valley to the Great Bend, past Furnace Run, to Pleasant Valley, and the village of Botzum. East of here are tortuous watercourses among the tumbled hills, but a gentler slope leads west to the brink of the valley. The Great Bend appears abruptly with the Portage Path and the old steps of locks began immediately, close to the mouth of the Little Cuyahoga.

Southwest of Akron at Summit Lake the canal led southwestward, joining the Tuscarawas at New Portage just northeast of Barberton. Thence it led along the west bank of that still small stream through a gentle valley to Clinton and Canal Fulton. From there on it enters a suggestion of a gorge past Crystal Spring to Massilon and then traverses the wide expanse drained by the broadening Tuscarawas and upper Sugar Creek. This brings it to Navarre set among broken hills and a narrowing valley trending westward.

Here the canal runs through the last undulations of the Alleghenies where the Tuscarawas cuts down to its wide junction with the Big Sandy. At Bolivar (Fort Laurens) and the mouth of the Sandy, it cuts across a wide loop of the Tuscarawas and clinging to the western hills, passes Zoar, and at Zoar Station enters the southerly gorge between Valley Junction and Dover. Here a conservation dam stands where one still sees the old canal bed.

Dover lies in a gateway to the wider Tuscarawas valley augmented by the waters of Sugar Creek. Here we see remote conical hills approaching the size of mountains, but the valley flat is wide. We pass New Philadelphia across the river, Old Schoenbrunn, Goshen, the home of Zeisberger, and come to Midvale and Tuscarawas. Uhrichsville lies eastward in the wide gap made by the Stillwater.

The next places of note are Gnadenhutten, then Lock Seventeen, then Port Washington and Newcomerstown. We are now travelling westward toward Coshocton, past the Blue Hole, a noted widewater. We continue westward in a prairie with distant hills through West Lafayette and Canal Lewisville, and then cross the inflowing Walhonding at Roscoe, turning abruptly south across from Coshocton. The Walhonding is a defile to the west, and high hills back Coshocton; the route ahead is southward through a straight, wide valley.

Now the canal clings to the western hills, with the river meandering far off in the meadows, past Adams Mills to Trinway in the flats north of Dresden. These are the prairies at the junction of Waketomika Creek and the Muskingum, for we have left the Tuscarawas behind at Roscoe. Here we leave it to the east and cross the Waketomika at Frazeysburg, passing between isolated conical hills in the flats to Nashport on the Licking. This is a region where old river courses have intermingled in the past. Westward, on the north side of the Licking, we soon enter the Black Hand Narrows at Toboso, a

51

lengendary spot and highly scenic. Soon we emerge into the upper, wider valley where Newark stands at the confluence of many streams, a natural gathering place for early primitive men as shown by the earthworks remaining.

Gradually ascending, we go southwestward past Four Mile Lock to Hebron on the Licking Summit. Eastward we see the long height of Flint Ridge bounding the Licking on the south and marked by the sentinel hill called Buzzards Glory Knob. We are on the National Road, Zane's Trace and U.S. 40. Just south lies the feeder pond for the old canal, Buckeye Lake, which in early days was known as the Big Buffalo Swamp.

From the Summit the canal descended gradually down a long steady slope to Lockville on the Little Walnut. The course now turns westerly around the headwaters of the Little Walnut to Lockbourne on the Big Walnut. We cut across a loop of this stream and come close to the Scioto, but continue onward, crossing the Walnut near Ashville, then finally cross the Scioto on the famous aqueduct. Here southeastward loom Mount Logan and other blue hills about the Pickaway Plains.

We descend the wide, flat valley until, at Westfall, we are abreast the northern part of the Plains, and crossing Deer Creek we come to Chillicothe at the mouth of Paint Creek. This is the most panoramic section on the route. The canal now continues close to the river and the western hills as far as Higby, and then veers to the southwest through Waverly and past Piketon across the valley. It crosses various westerly streams including Big Sunfish Creek and the Scioto Brush

52

Creek on a southerly course until it reaches Portsmouth across a wide flat at the confluence with the Ohio. Here was the other busy terminus of the canal, where for untold ages the Red Man had crossed the Ohio on his way to the Lakes. The great Warrior's Path followed up the Scioto to Sandusky Bay, but the canal was obliged to combine many old Indian routes to find water for its busy locks.

Returning to Carroll above Lockville on this route, we come to the junction of the Ohio and Erie and the Hocking Canals. We are upon the long westward slope of the tributaries of the Scioto and close to the summit near the headwaters of the Hocking. The Hocking Canal descended the deepening water crouse to Lancaster, lying among the isolated tors cropping out of the undulating land. The route descends more deeply to Logan, and then meanders through sharp ridges and narrow valleys to Athens among its complicated pattern of hills. Here the route ended, not attaining the broader valley and Hockingport, although between Athens and that river town the roads were well beaten at an early day.

Back at Lockbourne and northwards we follow the Columbus feeder. This is a slow, gentle rise up the wide, flat Scioto Valley, with a view of far hills to the eastward in the Walnut headwaters.

If we retrace our first route back through Lockbourne and over the Summit, we pass again through Newark and the Black Hand Narrows, behind the northern ridge of the National Road. We come to Dresden near the mouth of the Waketomika. This is the wide valley of the Muskingum

again, backed by high hills enclosing the wide waters of the combined Muskingum and Licking at Zanesville. Below this city the hills grow ever higher, and the valley seems narrower as we approach Marietta; yet the river itself grows deeper, and we are impressed by it, for it is a stream definitely navigable in the terms of early steamboating.

Imagine that you were going to make the full journey between Cleveland and Porstmouth or Toledo to Cincinnati. If you did not reside close to the canal you had to travel to the waterway by unimproved roads, which in bad weather were frequently very difficult because of mud and the scarcity of bridges over the smaller streams. In those days the distance which would be traversed in a day depended upon how far a horse could travel. The canals were actually so far apart within the State of Ohio that fifteen or twenty miles of travel was about all that could be done in a conveyance, in a day, although a man in the saddle could do better than that. For a family to travel far would mean that such a group would probably stay overnight at some intermediate point before reaching the canal.

If a bridge were out and the roads bad, the candlelight or the glow of a whale-oil lamp from some wayside travern or farmhouse might have proved a welcome sight on a dark night; and the coming of a gaily-painted packet on the canal may have signified as much to the traveller of that day as the train whistling for a way station did to a later generation. No doubt the smooth gliding motion of the packet or barge and the shifting glimpses of the canal-side life came as a pleasant relief from the jolting of wheels over rutted roads through a lonely countryside. What we read of crowded cabins and three tiers of hammock bunks may not have been a hardship in cool weather, and in all probability there were seasons in the year and stretches of the canal where there existed favorable opportunities for an exceedingly pleasant form of travel if speed were no requisite.

We can picture the appearance of the locks and landing stages where passengers would embark. A wooden platform might be found beside some widewater with steps leading down to the average level of the deck, or perhaps people merely stepped from the lock walls into the doorway of the cabin or upon the roof, from which they could find the cabin by a stairs. Boatmen would perhaps carry the satchels, carpetbags and small leather trunks across a plank and deposit these burdens in some portion of the cabin reserved for the purpose. Children in the quaint miniature grown-up costumes then in vogue would tease to remain on the roof deck to see all the activity of the locking through, and parents, unaccustomed to the experience, would be solicitous for their safety, for there were no rails on canal boats. It is even likely that curt and impatient suggestions would come from the crew, who would be busy with mooring ropes and pike poles as long as a boat was near a lock. The references left to us of the testimonials paid to captains for their courteous service to travellers are proof that such travellers were familiar with some standard of comparison.

If packets carried express freight, we cannot expect to visualize this packaged as such freight would be today. The almost universal container for everything but bulk material was the barrel, cask, keg or bale; the hogshead was also employed in many ways, and specially-made cases were not used before the age of mass production. The cargo seen by those who travelled on the slower barges would have added to the interest aroused—the great number of sacks of flour and wheat, the gypsum and the potash.

Those who have seen the stops made by river boats on the Ohio River will have some conception of the picture. These boats swing out a stage and make landings for the delivery or the taking off of freight from almost anywhere along the banks. On the canal the picture was in miniature, except that the water scene was reduced to almost nothing and the distance from boat to bank was a mere step.

Perhaps it was when the packet moved steadily through pastures and fields, occasionally shaded by overhanging trees, that one experienced to the fullest the charm of this form of transportation. In those days even the town man lived close enough to nature to participate in the interest the farmer felt in growing crops or scenes of the harvest; the canal was, to a great degree, a phase of agriculture. With the musky perfume of wheat in the hatches and other odorous cargo such as smoked ham and casks of cheese, there must have been a homeliness and intimacy in the stmosphere.

The people in our region were then almost without the social distinctions now existing; such differences as they recognized would scarcely be perceptible to us. We do know that all the waterways gave opportunity to the enterprises of the "rascals" of the day—the gamblers, the counterfeiters, the thieves—but, upon what was then almost the frontier of

56

the nation, they moved among others in a garb and manner undistinguishable from their fellows.

It was a homespun age. Beards and whiskers under the chin make all men look alike, and the dress of women in calico and bonnets, might not reveal the subtle differences in any manner indicative of social caste. Besides all this, the intimacy of such travel would not have tolerated any behavior denying the more nearly universal democracy of the time. With the coming of the railroads and the sifting of the population into grades of wealth, much of this surface quality was bound to cease, but the travel by barge or packet was largely a matter of cash on hand; whether on short hauls or through traffic, the passengers were all of one class.

Some people slept on deck in pleasant weather, especially if the boats were crowded. We hear of ague, of mosquitoes, of grounded boats and of floods; but, at a time when life was generally hard and full of unpredictable misfortunes, the experience of a journey by canal was sufficiently novel to provoke the traditional philosophy and good humor so evident in all the printed comments of the day. This is a form of humor differing from ours. Its stilted literary form in print could hardly have reflected its first spontaneous expression. This was Yankee humor, well seasoned with Gaelic and Teutonic flavoring. It had not the stereotyped sophisticated character which our present civilization demands today. It was ironical, sarcastic, but counterbalanced by a sentimentality almost naive yet frankly natural.

Architecture along the banks of our canals was much alike throughout the western region. In the Western Reserve it

tended perhaps toward a somewhat severe and solid Doric in all frame structures. The large doorways to warehouses or tavern stables had the characteristic cut-off upper corners; the windows were shuttered, and the gables had re-entrant angles. The wide, flat frieze plank was also employed. Down-state in Ohio there was often a suggestion of the Southern style, with pillared portico and dormer windows.

The canal days saw the building of many brick structures taking the form of the Pennsylvania type with two chimney flues at each end—the gables being on the sides with respect to the principal doorway. These gables did not usually carry a frieze, but were built up from the eaves in steps to the chimney level. There was often a frieze across the front under the eaves. In this kind of building there was little basic difference in the general aspect of a dwelling, warehouse, or church, as far as the essentials of the structure went; but charming spires appeared above the treetops whenever a church was built.

In many places, particularly along the Ohio and Erie Canal, these buildings often appeared above the canal on some hillside, lending charm to the background of the vista seen by the travellers from the lock or level. In the flatter country, long ranges of such buildings grew up along the towpath after the canal came. Many such essentially American scenes were mirrored in the still waters of the canal or loomed indistinctly through the mists to the eyes of the early-rising packet traveller.

There were many enterprises holding little attraction for us in their modern form—for instance, the marketing of cattle from the farms. In those days the drover came, pur-purchased his stock, and drove them east to York State. No doubt many a voyager by canal boat saw the herds on towpath or side road, lowing as they strayed, and held in check by a faithful watchdog. Again, he may have seen the cradler working in the wheat field or heard the whack of flails upon the threshing floor as he passed by.

No doubt the captain of the packet in his gold-buttoned blue jacket and peaked cap, leaning upon his tiller bar, inspired the ambition of many a small boy on his first voyage by canal; or perhaps the lad longed to be a lock tender, so awesome at his high post on the gates. The tender stood there like some St. Peter at his portal, lesser beings thrust upon the levers at his command.

Perhaps the most thrilling sight of all in the 1830's would be the chain of locks near a portage summit. Here the picture would be duplicated and its details multiplied, and its background would be topographically more complex. The summit meant a change of direction in the angle of the gates, a reverse flow to the water in the spillways, and a new and different aspect to the countryside. One coming to the Akron Summit would see a long and winding stairs of spurting locks give way to a wide and flattened landscape.

During the relatively short period between the first settlement of the state and the completion of the canals and railroads, a great number of stage lines carried passengers between towns on main turnpikes and secondary roads. These routes changed as canals or railroads were slowly completed, sometimes in detached sections.

Thus canals and stage lines worked together before the railroads came to serve the travelling public, and in a way the canals played their part in locating many marts of trade at crossroads not too far from their courses. Numbers of wagons always gathered about locks, mills and taverns, and these centers were in communication with others on the highlands round about. One such emporium was the old Whitcraft Store at Bath, west of the Cuyahoga on the old state road, U.S. 21. Places of this sort dealt with commodities carried by canal packets and barges, and at that time it was not necessary to drive the twenty to thirty miles to town, as such dealers were forced to do later, even after the coming of the railroads. Canal service was comparatively cheap. On the canal every lock was a station, and no stops could be eliminated for the sake of speed. The railroads soon discriminated between these settlements and created larger centers farther apart, leaving small communities to slumber in the lethargy afflicting the dying canal trade.

All along the Ohio and Erie Canal and in its immediate vicinity there are still many small family burying plots and individual graves dug during the earlier agricultural period of our history. Old settlers used to say that the population of the townships was much denser before the Civil War than after the subsequent development of the big cities.

The course of this canal and the remaining traces of its wharfs and warehouses provided a partial record of the economic life of the period. One of the first innovations occasioned by its building was the wider use of coal, made accessible south of the watershed—a fact that actually hastened its decline, since coal was essential to the development of the railroad. This was not foreseen at first because wood was so generally used as engine fuel. Yet the canal also reached places favorable for the production of building stone, pottery, ship timbers, barrel staves, lime and bricks—not to mention easy access to the harvest of the grain fields. It was many years before all this could be gathered in by the railroads.

60

CHAPTER SIX

The Miami-Erie-Wabash Canal

We now follow Lake Erie north of the watershed and toward the Maumee Valley. This watershed, close to the lake at Cleveland, bears off southwestward into the rolling hills of Ashland and Richland Counties, where the waters forming the Walhonding River are mustered to flow down to Coshocton and make the Muskingum and the Tuscarawas. But we keep on westward past the wide Sandusky–Scioto Gap to the mouth of the Maumee River. The Miami and Erie Canal, the rival of the Ohio and Erie, leads up the northwest bluff of this valley, traversing the basin of an ancient extended Lake Erie all the way to Defiance. The Wabash Extension continues within the same basin far into Indiana. In all this distance there are no far hills to be seen, only picturesque rapids, wooded islands, and distant level woodlands. The high watershed is far away to the southward beyond the old Black Swamp.

If we ascend the Auglaize by the old Miami Canal route, we mount slowly but steadily and pass the summit of the watershed at Loramie and St. Marys. We have no impression of the elevation, unless we go east to the heights of Bellefontaine and look down into the swift headwaters of the Mad River eastward.

From Piqua onward the descent is equally gradual and steady, down through Dayton and Middletown, until far hills draw in and the Miami Valley deepens. We pass through narrow Mill Creek and find Cincinnati seated on its steep hills on the Ohio.

The Mad River, west of the Scioto, rises but a short distance east of Ohio's highest point at Bellefontaine and cuts down very rapidly from the watershed through Urbana and Springfield to Dayton where it joins the Miami. This is a region of rolling hills quite unlike the rougher jagged character of those in eastern Ohio. The long course of the Ohio River along the southern edge of the State lowers the drainage level considerably, so the general effect is as though Ohio were tilted from northeast to southwest insofar as the land south of the watershed is considered. The northwestern section of the state may be said to slant to the northeast.

It is but a short distance west of Bellefontaine that we find the reservoir of the canal, Indian Lake. Further south, on this high plateau is Lake St. Marys and the Loramie Reservoir which provide the water for the long descent of the canal to Cincinnati. The main river begins at Indian Lake, flows southward for about twelve miles to DeGraff, and then westerly about ten miles to Port Jefferson. Thence the course of the feeder on the north bank of the river is generally southwest past Lockington to Piqua. Lockington lies on relatively high land between the Miami and Loramie Creek on the east side of the latter, and a sluice from the canal fell into the Miami north of Piqua at the western part of a bottom land. We come upon this neighborhood quite suddenly from the general levels eastward and it is the actual beginning of a much more scenic part of the lower Miami and Erie.

Below Piqua the valley widens and islands are formed in the river bed. The canal passed through the center of Troy and Tippecanoe City to the wide confluence of the Miami, Stillwater and Mad Rivers, after crossing the Miami halfway from Tippecanoe. Now following close to the eastern bluffs it

passed through Miamisburg, Franklin and Middletown opposite a two-mile flat at the two latter places. It swung to the southwest to Hamilton, and then southeast up a gentle declivity to Port Union. From the point where it left the Miami at Hamilton the rise to the reservoirs at Port Union was only about thirty feet. The channel then joined the East Fork of Mill Creek at Sharonville and followed down the west side at a high level to Lockland, Cumminsville and downtown Cincinnati, describing a course which lay close to the eastern foothills of the creek after crossing this at Carthage, three miles below Lockland.

The Miami Canal has no striking features north of the Loramie Summit except the impression of a low country charm east of Lake St. Marys, two widewaters a few miles north of that place, and a deep cut through a rolling ridge south of Spencerville. There is scarcely a bend in the channel through the Delphos Quadrangle, but there is a long trend to the northwest beginning at the confluence of the Blanchard with the Auglaize which takes the channel through the old Indian lands and villages on the latter river. Junction, where the Wabash Division joined, is the westernmost point of this trend, after which the canal strikes northeast to Defiance about nine miles away.

The abandoned Wabash Division still shows on the south side of the road from Junction through Antwerp. This former lake bottom has semicircular low elevations at various distances from the end of Lake Erie as a radial point; these mark old benches and glacial ridges, but they are not particularly distinct to the casual eye, nor of sufficient height to

Drivers' Duel on the Miami and Erie

Lock, Ohio and Erie

Opening Vista

Packet at Port Washington

Skating on Widewater

Reconstruction Over the Cuyahoga at Peninsula

Lost Lock

Lower Level

force the canal channel to deviate. Rather the canal followed the loops of the Maumee within Ohio, meandering more or less regularly along a straight line.

The Miami and Erie Canal took advantage of the most favorable conditions in the state for a canal. It was even possible to utilize the river as a waterway from Grand Rapids on the Maumee to near Texas. Three rivers fed the channel from Defiance down, and three large reservoirs on the Summit—Lake St. Marys, Loramie, and Indian Lake—carried the canal both north to Defiance and south to Piqua. Various dams and feeders made it possible to use the Miami as a feeder to Hamilton, and reservoirs above Mill Creek took it up and down to Cincinnati. The short Whitewater Canal connecting Cincinnati with Indiana was fed by streams from that state.

In contrast to the northern part of the Ohio and Erie, the Miami and Erie along the Maumee had the advantage of a tremendous drainage system extending far back into Indiana beyond Fort Wayne. Although there were no definite lakes on the Loramie Summit, it was possible to create the three artificial reservoirs out of large swamps in this widest part of the watershed.

The summit at Loramie is, perhaps, less apparent as a divide when approached from the north than it is when approached from the south. We find the upper Miami cutting through an abrupt valley with bluffs but no rolling hills behind. Perhaps it is the sluice pouring over the bluff above Piqua which gives the impression of water falling from a height of land when we come from this direction. Just above

this place the valley curves to the eastward with slanting ridges merging with the valley bottom, and this narrows as it approaches the comparatively level region around Indian Lake. Then, too, the high elevation east of Bellefontaine makes the neighborhood resemble bottom land rather than a table with a high average elevation.

Dayton and Hamilton are both situated in the widened valley bottom of the Miami. Hamilton is approached by the canal across a wide, flat from which the foothills appear quite remote. Dayton seems to be more hemmed in by the hills. From the latitude of the Mill Creek headwaters, the Miami makes a rapid fall down to the Ohio which is much deeper than Lake Erie. Thus it is that the approach to this summit is less apparent from the north than from between crowding hills adjacent to the Ohio.

The eastern feeder for the Miami Extension rose from a dam at Port Jefferson, four miles northeast of Sidney on the upper Miami.

Owing to the height of the banks of the Maumee, the streams on the north side, where lay the canal, either backed up against the canal bed to form widewaters against the foothills or were carried under its bed in deep culverts into the river. One of the largest of these widewaters was formed just east of Texas, where formerly great quantities of timber were stacked up waiting for the barges. Many of these barges were also "laid up" here for the winter. Another widewater existed to the west, near the famous old trading post recently torn down; this building stood immediately on the canal.

There were several towns, mostly on the northern bank,

63

created by the construction of the canal. Some of these were named after states holding the public interest at the time—California lies below Defiance. In addition to these aspects of the canal are those concerning Wayne's famous winter campaign against the Indian Confederation in Ohio and Indiana. Whereas the river towns are now somnolent, they were once busy, and much of their former picturesqueness remains. There is a monument beside the highway that occupies most of the old bed, commemorating the completion of the section and bearing the name of the contractor Durbin, who so ably did his bit and who now is buried in Texas in the village burial ground.

The canal towns on the Miami and Erie Canal were full of charm, considering that much of the landscape was relatively flat. The Maumee is full of tree-clad islands and rocky rapids. Part of it was made slack water by two dams, one above Grand Rapids and the other below Defiance. The river is used as a canal from the Grand Rapids Dam up to a point near Texas, where the canal then follows the top of the high bank to Defiance, where it entered Lock 1 in the center of the town, just above the old fort at the confluence.

Another charm, which still exists whether the canal is wet or dry, is found in the tremendous old sycamores, willows and other trees that grew up after this very early canal was built. The bank is high enough that panoramic vistas of the river reaches can be seen in many places.

The canal must have appeared in a striking aspect at Toledo where, as it turned into the Swan Creek Valley, it locked down a steep slanting course to the mouth of the creek

in the center of the city. The Maumee Canal, after passing Grand Rapids to the south, continued on very high land behind the Field of Fallen Timbers and a long way from the river until it met Swan Creek at Toledo. In many places along the Maumee this canal appeared high above the brink of the stream where the earth dug from its bed was strewn like a great talus slope down to the water. The mule teams pulling the boats would have been striking but minute figures on the skyline as seen from the river.

The works on the Miami and Erie Canal are exceedingly impressive. In many places the canal is carried over great fills, with the water responsible for side bays running in numerous culverts deep beneath the artificial bed of the canal. The construction of the Maumee section of this canal was, however, made easier by the fact that the river could be used between the Grand Rapids Dam and a lock below Texas. At Toledo the canal approached the town far from the river and was carried for some distance on the hillside above Swan Creek before it locked down into the Maumee in the center of the town.

The canal required occasional aqueducts, which meant a reasonably watertight and lengthy box of wood supported on stone or timber piers; this structure had to carry fully as much water as the channel proper. Since there was always a certain amount of leakage from these aqueducts, they tended to develop a picturesque drapery of green water weeds and moss, harmonizing them with their setting, although it was no evidence of their efficiency.

A common feature of the Maumee–Miami Canal was the

side-cut, where the canal was locked down directly into the river, for a time serving for the canal bed until the slack-water dam was reached and the canal was resumed. The exit of one side-cut existed a few miles below Texas and the re-entrance was made at the dam at Grand Rapids. Across the river at this place another short canal led into a basin at Grand Rapids. A sluice from the canal emptied into the river north of Maumee. This was a mile or more long and cut deeply into the earth near the river.

Keelboats passed up the Miami Valley very early in its history. Cincinnati had long been a focal point in the earliest days of settlement and a base of military operations. All through this period flour, bacon, and whisky had been carried up the river, and pelts and venison brought down from the wilds of the upper valley. When settlement had been well established, the fact that the stream was navigable for boats of considerable draft naturally brought about consideration of the possibilities of a canal, especially as canals were being planned elsewhere.

Dr. Daniel Drake launched the first campaign, and a preliminary survey for the Miami Canal was made in 1822. In 1824 a line was surveyed from Loramie to St. Marys, and by way of Cynthiana and Loramie Creek to the Great Miami; along that river to Jackson's Creek, seventeen miles above Dayton; to Dayton via the Mad River Valley; to Cincinnati by way of Middletown and Mill Creek Valley. Two lines were run down to Cincinnati—one to the upper plain without locks until near the Ohio, and the other locking down Mill Creek past the western part of the upper plain and to the lower plain of the city. The present High Level was finally selected. It was planned to terminate the canal at Deer Creek and let the High Level create water power.

After the necessary preliminaries to charters and financial means had been discussed, a charter was granted in 1825. Governor DeWitt Clinton (of New York), assisted by Governor Morrow (of Ohio), presided at the formal opening and dug the first spadeful at the Doty Lock on the farm of Daniel Doty, a mile and a half below Middletown. Work commenced near the mouth of the Mad River at Dayton, and a ditch was started down the river to Hamilton and via Mill Creek to Cincinnati. The section from Dayton to Cincinnati was 67 miles long, and it was completed in 1828.

In the first section of the Miami and Erie Canal were nine locks, five aqueducts, twenty culverts of three to twenty-foot chord, paved weirs, and road bridges. Later a feeder was built to draw water from the Miami above Middletown, and a side-cut was made to connect Hamilton with the system. The first boat, a packet of the Farmer's and Merchant's Line, arrived at Cincinnati in May, 1827. P. A. Sprigman was the captain. The opening of this canal was, like that of the Ohio and Erie, marked with great pomp and circumstance, with the Cincinnati Guards and Hussars representing the military.

Some difficulty was expected and later was actually experienced in carrying the Miami Canal over the Mill Creek Summit. It is registered in old contracts that the filling of the channel cut off old out-flows from the swamps on that irregular ground. It would seem that the carrying of the channel above portions of the natural level resulted in more trouble than digging below it would have been. Water both within and without the banks kept these in a state of instability and saturation. One of the difficulties with the water supply lay in evaporation, another in lock leakage, and yet another in the intrusion of storm water.

The Miami, Wabash and Erie Canal was built in independent sections which were later joined to form the entire system. The Miami actually began with the breaking of ground at Main Street, Cincinnati, on July 21, 1825. It was finished up to the Miami Feeder on July 1, 1827, but many of the new banks soon caved in. By November 28, 1827, boats began to reach Middletown. The 67-mile section from Cincinnati to Dayton was being used in 1828. Rainy seasons checked much of the early work, causing many overflows and bringing many damage suits to the Company. The new canal earned $8,707 the first year, and in ten years showed an annual gross of $81,431. The line was completed as far as Piqua, forty miles from Dayton, in 1840, and up to the junction with the Wabash section in 1848.

The construction of the Hamilton Basin was awarded to Andrew McCleary, a subcontractor, who paid 30 cents a day to laborers or 75 cents a day to men who could furnish a team. In spite of the seemingly low wages he paid, the loss was $1,500 on a $7,500 job. This basin, which was five feet above the level of the town, leaked badly after it was finished, and a drain was made south of the Square to the river. The dimensions of the basin were as follows: 120 feet wide at the bottom; 148 feet wide at the surface; depth 18 feet, making 5 feet of the depth above the natural level. This basin leaked

66

for years, since the two towns then existing would not cooperate in repairing it.

The new basin built for the canal became a center of activity, for 71 boats arrived and 77 left in April, 1829. It is said that gravel tended to fill the lower levels near Hamilton after the canal was opened. Stone for locks on the Miami Canal was found at the C. K. Smith quarries above Roseville and at the R. B. Millikin quarries at the lower end of Roseville. During the first years of operation the Miami Canal was frozen up to seven weeks at a time, and the needed repairs hampered navigation. When steam dredges came, much time was saved.

The first packet company on the Miami Canal built splendid boats, painted white; there were deck awnings, window shutters, red silk curtains, fine interior upholstery and comfortable bunks. The service was most thoughtfully planned for the convenience and entertainment of passengers; five excellent meals were served between Dayton and Cincinnati, a Negro fiddler provided music for dancing on the roof, and even the horses wore bells and ribbons.

James Steele and Henry Bacon rode through the woods to Newark at the time of the Ohio Canal opening to invite the Governor to Dayton to boost the canal project there. The Governor accepted this invitation and attended a famous dinner at the Compton Tavern on Second Street. One plan was to dig the canal down Main Street, which some considered a beautiful idea. The original plan put Dayton at the head of navigation for keelboats, and the basin at Second Street was usually crowded. The completion of the canal did away with this scene, for the last keelboat left in 1828 and the warehouse was eventually washed away by high water.

There was some inevitable dissatisfaction with the management of the canals. The state did not purchase all land outright, but made awards for damages in excess of benefits derived from the use of canals, and property owners were paid for earth excavated for the building of banks. No fences could be built closer than fifteen feet to the inner line of the towpath, making the right of way seventy feet wide. Three Commissioners met periodically to discuss claims. They received $3.00 a day as pay which was later raised to $3.50. They paid their own transportation and expenses.

An old photograph taken in Dayton shows a lock and sluice south of the Jefferson Street canal bridge. This has a single stone arch.

The Miami Extension was the section built after the Canal had been finished as far as Dayton. This crossed the Mad River a mile above that city on an aqueduct, and bridged the Miami above on six stone arches, then passed through ten locks to reach Tippecanoe, Troy, and Piqua; thence through nine locks at Lockington where the Sydney Feeder entered. At the Loramie Feeder it entered a section where it was taken down by eleven locks to the St. Marys level with a feeder from Lake St. Marys. From this place there were twenty-one locks in the fifty miles to Junction where the canal joined the Wabash and Erie, a short distance south of Defiance.

In the vicinity of Defiance there were nine locks, after which there was a long stretch of twenty-three miles through Napoleon to a lone lock at Texas. Halfway to Providence there were two more locks down to the two-mile level at Maumee, which was a distance of eight miles, and two more locks to Toledo. At Toledo six locks took the level down to that of Swan Creek after the section to Manhattanville through the city was abandoned.

The Loramie Reservoir was completed in 1844. This is the site of Loramie Station, a trading post of one Pierre Loramie in early Indian days. Indian Lake, or Lewiston Reservoir, was made by placing a dam over the Miami headwaters west of Bellefontaine; a feeder canal led from near this place down to the Loramie Dam near Piqua.

Work had begun at Piqua in 1833 and the division was finished June 20, 1837. The "Emigrant" was launched the following day and was the first boat to pass through the Piqua lock. On June 22 a small boat arrived from Northumberland, Pennsylvania, with pleasure seekers for Loramie. It had to be portaged between Troy and Culbertson lock. This party joined in the opening celebration which followed.

A buckeye was planted in Main Street, with a flag and seasonal flowers in front of the National Hotel, on July 4, 1837. There was a three-day celebration of the event. A boat came from Dayton to Troy with General Harrison. There was also the "Clarion," Captain Owen, and the "Emigrant" of Piqua accompanied the "Clarion" back as far as Adam's lock.

It is reported that those property owners of Piqua on the west side of the canal between Ash and Greene Streets made a basin on their land with a 30-foot wide wharf which became Canal Street. Many boats came down the Ohio [River] from

67

Portsmouth and up the Miami and Erie Canal to Piqua. These boats were able to run through to Lake Erie on the Miami Extension after 1844.

The enthusiasm of the people of northwestern Ohio over the possibilities of a canal system did not lag behind that of the citizens of eastern Ohio. A survey was made along the Maumee and Auglaize, and to the Wabash as early as 1824. There was good reason for this as the Maumee was considered navigable to large craft as far up as Swan Creek at Toledo. The difficult Ohio–Michigan boundary dispute held up all decisions in the matter for a decade. In 1834 it was proposed to dam the river and use slack water for steamers as far as Defiance, and to continue the rest of the way to Fort Wayne with the use of canal boats. It was believed that a steam tug could tow two canal boats from Defiance as far as the Rapids, and carry the horses as well. This was figured as cheaper than to use them on a 40-foot canal.

John Wood obtained the land grants for the extension of the Miami Canal to include the Maumee Valley. His newspaper boosted this canal campaign. It is said that the Canal Commission encouraged cash payments for a better grade of flour than could be obtained by barter. Money was scarce, and this practice immediately resulted in improved quality in products.

Considering the nature of the river below the Rapids, Toledo, Perrysburg, and Maumee City all wanted to control the mouth of the proposed canal; even Manhattan at the mouth of the Bay wished to do the same. Finally a Commission meeting at Perrysburg decided to carry the course all the way to Manhattan, and give Maumee a side-cut canal. This side-cut was about equally favorable to Perrysburg, since both towns are nearly opposite and below the Rapids on slack water at the lake level. The first contract for construction was let at Maumee in 1837. Two thousand laborers were employed. They were paid in Michigan "wildcat" bills, borrowed for the purpose. There was a financial panic in 1837, and contractors had trouble over a nonpayment of wages for five months. The stores issued due bills which were paid in June of that year.

July, 1838 saw work on the Wabash and Erie advancing through that wilderness region. The *Defiance Banner* predicted a canal from Lake Erie to the Indiana line within a year and a rich wheat business in Indiana's "second Egypt." R. H. Backus of Cleveland announced more canal boats, horses and harness put in his charge for sale, and boats to be had with or without horses.

Much of the line of the Wabash and Erie Canal was completed by January 26, 1841, with the exception of the reservoir near the Indiana line. The first boats to get to Cleveland in April of that year were the "Ontario," F. Worcester, Captain, from Beaver, and the "John C. Hart" from Middlebury. In May the steamboat "Wisconsin" arrived from the Erie Canal. This boat name suggests the great wave of migration passing into Wisconsin via the Great Lakes.

By June, 1842, the Maumee Canal was opened from Toledo to the Rapids, and from Toledo to Fort Wayne on May 8, 1843.

The course of the canal up the Maumee was a well-beaten trail since the days of Anthony Wayne; but south through the Black Swamp the contractors met with difficulty, ten and a half miles southwest of Defiance at Junction in Paulding County, where the southern course divided from that leading to Fort Wayne. This part was called the Wabash and Erie, and the other the Miami and Erie. Eventually the first boat came from Cincinnati to Toledo on June 27, 1845. An important use was made of the Miami and Erie section in carrying soldiers from Toledo, Michigan and northwestern Ohio to the Mexican War—the officers being given the privilege of travelling by packet, while the enlisted men travelled on freight barges. The federal government considered this route an important military highway between New York and New Orleans until 1856.

In building this canal the laborers were well paid, and as it passed through cheap new land, many of them settled along the route. Over $3 million worth of produce entered Toledo via the canal in 1848, and $5 million worth was shipped through to the south.

Owing to the rapids in the Maumee there was the advantage of water power at the lower levels. The Rapids stretch for several miles between Grand Rapids and Maumee City, dotted with wooded islands, and passing the Roche de Bout and the Battlefield of Fallen Timbers. The canal traversed the top of the western bluff, gaining height above the river as it went. It was this fall that made it possible to utilize the water power wherever a ravine cut down from the plateau. At Maumee there was a considerable side-cut, leading down to a basin southwest of the town, which was employed as a port across from Perrysburg.

When business on the canal was at its peak, packets came from as far as the Erie Canal, some of them being very large. The largest of all was the "Harry of the West," Captain Edwin Avery, which came in 1844. These packets carried express freight and some U.S. mail. They were drawn by from two to six horses, hitched as teams, with the rider seated upon the left rear horse. The average speed of travel was from six to eight miles per hour, which of course could not be continuous, although there were relatively few locks to slow up progress.

The best time made by the packets was Toledo to Lafayette (Indiana), 242 miles in 56 hours. On June 28, 1847, the "Empire," Captain Wiggin, left Dayton and made Toledo, 180 miles, on the 29th in the morning. The passengers expressed their appreciation through a notice in the *Toledo Blade*. The fare was three cents a mile on packets and two and a half cents on the freight boats. Mails and lodgings were included on long trips.

To make the whole trip from Toledo to Cincinnati took four days and five nights, including the time needed to pass through the locks and to handle express freight at way points. It was only a short time before railroads turned the thoughts of the canal people to steam power. The first steam canal boat was the "Niagara," built in 1845 for Samuel Doyle at a cost of $10,000; but this failed to compete successfully with horses. The steamer "Scarecrow" was more successful, making its first trip to Franklin with lumber. It had a portable engine attached by a belt to a pulley on the drive shaft.

However, canal engineers were inclined to believe that steam propulsion stirred up too much commotion for the safety of other craft and damaged the banks with the wash.

Those familiar with the present boulevard in Toledo known as the Anthony Wayne Trail might not realize that this road occupies virtually the line of the old canal. This is especially true within the strip between Maumee and the City of Toledo.

The following is a description of the old Miami and Erie from the terminus to Manhattanville southward:

From the lower miter sill of the outlet lock at Manhattanville to the head of the side-cut into Swan Creek was five miles with a fifteen-foot elevation. There were two locks near the river. This extension was abandoned March 26, 1864.

The northern part of this section was occupied by the Wheeling and Lake Erie tracks to Cherry Street, thence nearly south over Oak Street at Allen, across Adams between Ontario and Michigan, Madison at Ontario, Jefferson nearer Ontario than Erie, Monroe nearer Erie, Washington at Erie, westward across Lafayette at Ontario, southward over Nebraska Avenue, just west of 13th and Swan Creek just east of Wyandott.

The connection with the lower Maumee was the Toledo side-cut which dropped fifteen feet into Swan Creek by two locks.

From the head of the Toledo side-cut, eleven miles from its entrance into Swan Creek, the canal rises 48 feet to Maumee, eight and five-sixth miles, by six locks to No. 9.

70

Here was the former side-cut to the river, a fall of 63 feet with six locks. This side-cut was abandoned about 1865.

Size of these locks was ninety by fifteen feet. Between Toledo and Junction (ten and a half miles southwest of Defiance), a distance of 69 miles, the prism was sixty by forty by six.

There were expansions at ports and at necessary intermediate points for turning. The extant canal, from Maumee side-cut at Lock 9 to the head of Grand Rapids, is fifteen and a half miles without a lock.

The State Dam is at Grand Rapids, two parts with an island between, one 66 and the other 1,700 feet. It is five and a half feet high. Here is guardlock No. 10, and boats run in slack water for one mile.

A large part of the Maumee River was used in lieu of canal. This was accomplished by the building of the dams—one at Grand Rapids and the other at Independence, a short distance below Defiance. The part actually used by the barges extended from a point a short distance below Texas to the dam at Grand Rapids, the Independence dam being built to form a high feeder for the long stretch down to Texas. From Grand Rapids the canal continued at a very high level all the way to Swan Creek in Toledo.

Locks 1 and 2 of the Auglaize section of the Miami Canal were directly upon the Maumee River at Defiance and just west of the mouth of the Auglaize. These were deep, wooden locks, for after leaving the Maumee, there is little local stone, so that many of the locks in that section were built of wood.

An interesting fact regarding the St. Marys Reservoir and

Feeder is found in *The History of Warren County*. The reservoir is nine miles long and two to four miles wide, and lies three miles west of the canal. There was a natural elevation on the north and south, and embankments ten to twenty feet high were made at the east and west. When this area was filled, the neighbors feared the miasma, and 150 men made a breach in these banks. An old drawing by Henry Howe shows the dead trees standing in the reservoir.

Celina stands at the west end of this artificial lake, and the area is large enough to hide the lower stages of the town from the east end. Like other reservoirs of this kind, one comes upon it quite unexpectedly.

The success of the Miami Canal led to the construction of the Whitewater Canal by a private company. This led from Cincinnati into Indiana via Whitewater Creek, and was originally planned to run from Cambridge City on the National Road to Lawrenceburg on the Ohio. Forty miles of this route were already completed. The connection was made at Harrison on the state line. The 25 miles from Cincinnati were predicted to be navigable the greater part of the year.

This canal proved to be very expensive to build and run. Competition and damage by floods discouraged its maintenance, and it was abandoned. Its terminal became railroad yards in Cincinnati.

The Whitewater Canal also entered the Ohio River between Cleves and North Bend through a tunnel nineteen feet long near Harrison's tomb.

Its bed in the city limits and Pearl Street Market was leased to the Cincinnati and Indianapolis Railroad after it was abandoned. The Plum Street Depot is near the old terminus. In "Cincinnati, a Guide to the Queen City" (Works Projects Administration, 1943), it is stated that the Whitewater Canal was built in the 1830's and was in operation between Cincinnati and Brookville, Indiana, in 1843. It was actually begun in 1834 and abandoned in 1863.

Back as far as June 17, 1853, the *North West* (Napoleon, Ohio) published the history of the Wabash and Erie Canal, considering it as quite ancient. The facts were as follows: Land was granted for the purpose in 1827, 1841 and 1845. Work was commenced in 1832, and was finished to Lafayette in 1841, to Covington in 1846, to Coal Creek in 1847, to Terre Haute in 1849, to Point Commerce in 1851 and to Evansville in 1853. The length of the canal in Indiana was 375 miles and in Ohio 81 miles—456 miles in all.

The subject of the Miami–Wabash and Erie Canal would not be complete without mention of the Western Reserve and Maumee road. Kathryn Miller Keller tells, in the *Northwestern Ohio Historical Quarterly* some of the many interesting facts regarding it. It seems that this was the "road with a tavern every mile," but not because the travellers wished to stop as often as that. It was because the road was so poor. It led through much of the old Black Swamp, and because it was not improved until 1839 it got a bad name, even though the mail and many adventurers and honest immigrants put it to constant use. The road was the result of the Treaty of Brownstown in 1808, and the Government reserved land 120 feet wide from the western boundary of the

Connecticut Reserve to the Maumee. It was surveyed by authority after December 21, 1811; alterations in the course were made in 1816 to take in the U. S. Reservation at Lower Sandusky or modern Fremont.

This famous road ended at Perrysburg, where the last of its thirty taverns was located, doubtless familiar to travellers upon the Miami Canal. There was also the Exchange Tavern on Front Street at Perrysburg, whence a famous tavern bell bell was stolen by Indians who were intrigued by its sound. They tied it to a horse to hear it ring, and so were easily apprehended.

Often one runs across reference to this road in connection with improvements upon the canals. Apparently it never received quite the same attention as the waterways, but it was just as important to travellers. It was comparatively late in the history of the State of Ohio that this northwestern region was fully developed, although the Miami Canal to the south was in use very early. The Blank Swamp was a formidable obstacle for roads, but it had the water for a canal. Paulding County remained a woods up to the time of the lessening of activity upon the Miami and Erie, and even later.

In some ways the imaginative picture which we can paint of the Miami Canal differs considerably from that of its sister waterway, the Ohio and Erie. The Red Man had already left the Cuyahoga and the Tuscarawas, but he remained about the Auglaize during almost the whole active life of the canals. The passage of the packets and barges along this waterway must have been an interesting penetration of

72

civilization into the wilds of a country that was almost unsettled.

The whole route of the Miami, Wabash and Erie is almost identical with that followed by Anthony Wayne, Arthur St. Clair and other military leaders of the early wars. It is the ancient highway of the first French traders who visited this region. The Miami River was the last and most important entrance into the Indian country, and the Maumee River was the earliest route into the Mississippi Valley used after settlements had been made by the French in Indiana and Illinois.

Fort Miami, built on the "Miami of the Lakes" just north of Maumee, is the oldest military site in Ohio. It was held by the British during Wayne's campaign. Almost across from it stood Fort Meigs of 1812, while Fallen Timbers, Roche de Bout, and Grand Rapids, a little above, played an interesting part in the two wars. It is particularly about Defiance that famous sites of frontier camps and incidents are to be found. Still, such things can be noted as far as the Wabash section can be traced.

Also, we must not overlook the fact that Cincinnati was a canal city, although it had already become great through the keelboat and the river steamers before canal days arrived. This far western river town and fort was known long before other Ohio cities had a name. From here had gone all the military expeditions to the north, while settlers followed them up the Miami Valley. Both the Miami and the Mad Rivers had been noted for their swiftness, and it was only natural that the canalization promised a much better means of continuing trade in the years of peaceful settlement.

Mill Creek afforded a shorter route and a safer one for entering the levels of the upper valley, and this old trail promised much water power from the canal. At Cincinnati, with its towering hills and its colorful life, we see the life of the canal joining another water-borne commerce quite different from that found by the Ohio and Erie at Cleveland. At the latter place were white-sailed schooners coming in from the blue lake. At Cincinnati the white barges locked down to a basin set between mountainous hills dotted with buildings, to moor alongside the gaily-fretted and high stacked river packets.

It would seem that the period between 1825 and 1842 saw the thriving youth of both canals, for after that era much comment centered rather upon the acts of politicians, toll rates, railroad competition, and the need for greater scope in the use of waterways. It is evident that the packet services discontinued as soon as railroads became established and the canal men settled down to the serious work of competing for the freighting business.

Sandy · Beaver Canal   The Big Tunnel.

CHAPTER SEVEN

The Sandy-Beaver Canal

Of all the canals built up to 1834 the story of the Sandy–Beaver reads the most romantically. It was a "lost cause" to which, in retrospect, we respond with sympathy often withheld from successful work. It was not the only canal which failed. Other failures were the Whitewater, the Warren County Canal, and the partially successful and much battered Hocking Canal. But the route of the Sandy–Beaver is beautiful, and all the events of its building and the sublime faith of its sponsors win respect—not to mention the obviously almost superhuman efforts exerted by the men who labored on it.

At the time the Sandy–Beaver was chartered, the Miami and Erie had been finished to Dayton, the Ohio and Erie was complete with a feeder to Columbus and the side-cut to Lancaster. The Pennsylvania and Ohio Canal was proposed. There was a canal from Beaver to New Castle on the Shenango, and, at the junction of the Mahoning and Shenango, was the connection with the proposed Pennsylvania and Ohio. The Pennsylvania Canal came to Freeport and then down the Allegheny to Pittsburgh.

There were three divisions to the Sandy–Beaver Canal, the Middle being precisely the Summit itself. This was fourteen miles long. It extended from a point a mile and a half west of New Lisbon to two miles below Hanover. The first six miles were level and a good soil was found. Two cuttings of a third of a mile each were required, with a depth of twelve feet. There was a second portion, four miles long, in the winding headwaters of the West Fork; there were two cuttings in this of 30 and 36 feet depth. The third portion of this Summit was two miles long and intersected the dividing ridge, requiring a tunnel of 900 yards, with cuttings at each end two and a quarter miles long and twenty feet deep on the average. Four shafts had been sunk for exploration. The height of the ridge was 120 feet, and the shafts were 89 feet deep. A rock excavation and a deep cut were required at the west end.

The Western Division was thirty-three and a half miles long from the first lock below Hanover to Bolivar. Here was a satisfactory set of circumstances with a lockage of 223 feet. One lock was required to raise the last level to that of the Ohio and Erie Canal. To supply this section with water there were two feeders and Sandy Creek itself. This required two dams four and a half feet high. The channel required three crossings by means of aqueducts, the last being over the Tuscarawas. Apparently the only difficulty on this section was three bluff banks requiring protection walls.

The Eastern Division made a rapid descent by locks to the Middle Fork, and the first plan was to carry it by the right bank of the Ohio to the Big Beaver and the Pennsylvania Canal (probably to terminate at the 43rd mile near the Beaver bridge.) The report called for 27 locks down from the Summit, with a lift of 6 feet each and 162 feet aggregate. It was planned to keep each lock independent of the other, with basins 86 feet long. These shelving basins from lock to lock would do away with the necessity of breast walls here. There was adequate stone for these locks at hand. The foot of this flight of locks would reach the Middle Fork, where a feeder was needed. The course was then to the left bank and

through New Lisbon to about five miles beyond, where there were favorable flats. It was planned to dam the lower river, thus forming slack-water pools one to three hundred rods long for five miles in nineteen. Only the construction of towpaths and dams was needed. This scheme was entirely impractical.

The section or prism of this canal was to be 40 x 28 x 4 feet and the locks 15 x 90 feet. On the Summit this profile was to be 40 x 28 x 7. The section of the tunnel was to be thirty square yards, except for two recesses 75 feet in length with a profile of fifty square yards. The towpath was to be discontinued through this tunnel. It was suggested that an endless chain be used to tow the barges here, with the use of stationary horse power.

Elderkin Potter, attorney of New Lisbon, was the leading spirit in the conception and the building of the Sandy–Beaver Canal. The first ground was broken on March 3, 1835, but the panic of 1837 suspended operations for a time. The canal was completed in 1846. The Summit level of this canal was fourteen miles long, with only sufficient water in reservoirs to maintain evaporation and leakage for six months of the year; the rest of the time it was frozen. In view of the immense amount of labor and capital expended the canal was a failure, yet the project had the immediate effect of distributing capital, tending to build up a local democratic spirit in the community, and furnishing a market for local enterprises during its building. The great numbers of laborers employed brought money to the hands of storekeepers and those providing lodging.

The Sandy–Beaver was apparently the only canal in Ohio not surveyed and engineered by the state. Merely as an achievement of engineering, it stands out as a great feat, especially for the building of the rock tunnel. But over-enthusiasm made wishful thinkers of those who must have known about the insufficiency of water on the divide. The system was operated for some time in two sections and transported some freight; but some say that only one boat ever made the full trip.

Beginning at Smith's Ferry at the mouth of the Little Beaver, we find the Sandy–Beaver ascending the exceedingly deep and narrow valley past Grimm's Bridge and Saint Clair at the mouth of the North Fork. It then escapes the closer confines of the hills, and winds tortuously through the high knobs of Saint Clair, Middleton and Elk Run townships, past Elkton to Lisbon. At this point it has almost reached the high plateau, but the region is irregular and cut by small watercourses. The canal now crosses the Middle Fork, along which it has proceeded at McKinley Crossing a short distance northwest of Lisbon, and continues north-westward through two marshes just east of Guilford; these were evidently the feeders of the summit level. By way of the West Fork the waters of the Watercress Marsh also entered the canal at Guilford; the west end of this marsh is also the source of the Mahoning River.

These marshes appear on the map to be rather extensive, but it is evident that they are shallow, as there is flat land all about. The general level here is about eleven hundred feet. Of course Lisbon people wanted a canal to pass through that

town; so the course of the canal does not take the direct route of the Great Trail of Indian days or other paths leading more directly from the Beaver to Fort Laurens at Bolivar. The foothills extending southwestward between Salem and Lisbon form an abrupt watershed, and it is questionable whether any other route, such as directly up the West Fork through West Point, would have provided any more water except through the use of a reservoir on a modern scale. Thus it was that the canal had to go southward down the west side of the West Fork for two miles, after which it went southwest to Dungannon in Hanover township where, a mile northeast, it passed through the short timbered tunnel at a surface elevation of about twelve hundred feet.

The canal joined Sandy Creek four miles west of Dungannon at Kensington after passing through the long rock tunnel about midway, at a surface elevation of 1,238 feet. On this portion of the highlands the map shows no ponds or marshes, the land being a complicated pattern of hills and small ravines. It was most unfortunate that this line of canal was not practical, for the route passes through some beautiful Ohio country and, to this point, is unique in canal topography. The lower reaches of all the Ohio tributaries are hemmed in by hills as high as those of the Ohio canal itself and, until Elkton is passed, the landscape is dramatically rugged. Toward Lisbon the lower hills are backed by high knobs and ridges rising in the blue distance, and then we come to the high rolling land of the watershed. The drop down West Fork takes us again into a region of steep hillsides and shaded bottoms about Dungannon and westward to the Sandy.

Lost Lock Above Grand Rapids

Boat in Lock, East of Texas

Retreating Shower, Miami Canal

Old Berme Bank, Texas

Maumee at Bad Creek

The Widewater.

Texas on the Maumee

Bad Creek Outlet at Texas

Widewater at Texas

Suggests former warehouse at Waterville.
Note change in loading pulley.

After passing through the long tunnel, the miniature Smoky Mountains of Columbiana are left behind, and the rounded slopes of the Sandy Valley appear. The channel can perhaps be seen at Malvern with its feeder dam. The Nimi-shillen was crossed at Sandyville by means of a dam to keep the level, a method peculiar to this canal.

As soon as the Sandy Valley is reached, the hills draw back and the bottoms widen; we get the impression that the streams emptying into the Sandy are not cut to the depths of the Beaver Forks. From Kensington we continue westward past East Rochester, Bayard, Minerva, and Malvern, passing many tributaries springing from the twelve hundred foot level in the hills about. Waynesburg, Magnolia, and Sandy-ville are passed, with the valley becoming steadily wider and deeper until we reach the terminus in the broad expanses around Bolivar.

The lower portion of the Sandy Valley gives us the impression of a terrain typically canal-like; but it is somewhat tame after coming out of the Columbiana Hills. However, the sudden width of the confluence is impressive. An old photograph of a canal boat shows the approach to the Big Tunnel on the Sandy-Beaver with the white barge reflected in the calm waters of the channel, and a high hill in sunset light blocking the view to the east. It is evident that the lower portion of the canal was the most profitable in its short history, since, from this point west, there was a more constant supply of water. Here the canal profited by the conditions enjoyed by the Ohio and Erie. It was unfortunate that those who most wanted the canal dwelt over in Lisbon where the rains ran off swiftly from the shallow marshes and flowed quickly down the deep ravines into the Ohio.

From the divide there were twenty-one locks down to the Little Beaver, eighty locks to the Ohio River, and sixty locks from the summit to the Tuscarawas. This is an astonishing number considering the distance in a straight line.

What a landscape was missed when this canal failed to become a travelled route! There was Guilford Lake and Pine Hill with a towpath fifty feet above one of the swiftest streams in Ohio. Before leaving the gorge of the West Fork, the canal entered the smaller timbered tunnel one hundred feet above the water. In this region were mills, covered bridges and houses now abandoned and ghostly. The entrance to the long rock tunnel has been blocked, and no living person has ever seen it. Water issues from the ground to form a pond before it. Here were the impediments of quicksand and rock falls which nature has covered over and redeemed.

Topographically considered, the Sandy–Beaver traversed an exceedingly rough and hilly region in Columbiana County and the rounded smooth Sandy Valley. There were fifteen locks in less than two miles north of Lisbon. The hilly nature of this region made it decidedly beautiful, though impractical; the country southward especially is noteworthy for its scenic character. One of the noted locks was Lusk's Lock (No. 2) built in 1836, and named after its contractor. It was 102 feet long, with 12 foot walls, 14 feet apart (one of the largest in the state), a beautiful piece of well-constructed masonry.

The Big Tunnel east of Hanover on the way to Dungannon

was nine hundred yards long with a deep cut at either end. It had a height of seventeen to eighteen feet and lay eighty feet below the Summit. To build it the blasted rock was lifted through shafts built on the course. A hundred and twenty-five men worked day and night from both ends of the excavation, and it took three years to build. Shack towns to house the Irish laborers were built up along the route, and local names still attest to this fact.

The Little Tunnel lay northeast of Dungannon. It was nearly a thousand feet long and was timbered, being dug through earth. This tunnel and a few locks let the canal down to the West Fork three or four miles below Guilford.

The Western division of the canal extended from Hanover to Bolivar, thirty-three and a half miles, and cost $10,000 a mile. It passed through Minerva, Malvern, and Waynesburg. There was a reservoir for this section on the Kensington (then Maysville). The Eastern division began at the Summit above Lisbon and followed the Middle Beaver through Elkton, Williamsport, and Frederickton; then by way of the Little Beaver to the Ohio at Smith's Ferry. The forty-three miles of this section cost $12,000 a mile. The entire cost of the canal was $1,144,000, and the entire length was ninety and a half miles, although the distance between the terminals is only half that distance in a straight line, owing to the tortuous hill and valley character of the eastern half. The Western division was made forty feet wide at the surface, twenty-eight at the bottom, and was four feet deep. There were forty locks between Hanoverton and Bolivar, and 140 from Hanover to Smith's Ferry. Obviously, in view of the

82

number of locks required on the Ohio and Erie, there were too many costly locks on this route for a quick paying off of the costs of construction.

The Sandy–Beaver Canal may be said to have been in operation for three years. The year 1854 was very dry on the divide, and boats went west from Hanover only. When this happened, it was decided to abandon the canal, and the "J. P. Hanna," grounded at Lynchburg, was left to rot away at that place.

The route of the Sandy–Beaver is rich in the lore and tradition of earlier days, and it has a natural background eminently suitable for the inspiration of the historian. At nearby Negley is the high isolated hill occupied by Boquet on his expedition to Coshocton. Up this route came the very earliest Indian traders, who later followed routes entering the then Indian Territory at points lower on the Ohio. This was the preferred route into the Tuscarawas Valley, striking almost due westward through the folds of the jumbled hills to the more open regions of the Sandy Valley. The canal passed through Dungannon, known at one time as Painted Post; this was a junction of forest trails and a lonely landmark in the wilderness east of the divide. From here paths led down into the lower Tuscarawas and eastward to the Mahoning. The forces coming to raise the siege of Fort Laurens passed by this way, and not far off this route Morgan the raider was captured while seeking a way to recross the Ohio.

The eastern section of the canal from Lisbon to the Ohio was kept up for some time; but the fundamental failure of the canal was a blow to the community, and many citizens left.

Famous landmarks of New Lisbon were the Bend of the Little Beaver, the McKinley, Vallandingham, and Hanna homes, and Lock Stone 27 which was set in the sidewalk of Market Street at a later day.

Stark County was naturally interested in the Sandy–Beaver project. Canton was unfortunately too far from a major stream to claim a main route, but the prospect of a canal a few miles south on the Sandy aroused the citizens to attempt the canal down the Nimishillen. This stream was too rapid and too small to afford the necessary conditions. The big plow and the many oxen used to pull it through Canton is a picturesque incident of canal history.

The point for the beginning of excavation on the Nimi-shillen Canal was at North Walnut Street, Canton. Shriver's Run was employed to keep the ditch filled. The fall of this channel in the short distance to the Sandy was so rapid that it was entirely impracticable, for this rate of fall would have required more locks per mile than existed in other canals for the same distance. But Canton had not long to wait for her place in the sun. The railroads came and proved much more profitable than the canal could ever have been.

One driving southwest of Salem on Route 9 will, in a short time, find himself meeting the first undulations of the Allegheny Uplift. Just north of New Garden he will cross the Watercress Swamp, lying in the folds of considerable hills. This marsh contains but little water, yet reveals some old stonework which may remain from a dam, either for a mill or as an adjunct to the feeders for the Sandy–Beaver Canal. This area embraces quite a few weedy acres with willows

growing in its lowest levels; it is the source of both the Mahoning and the West Fork of the Beaver. It has apparently returned to nature after earlier clearing.

At the top of the ridge to the south lies the hamlet of New Garden, and going east we come abruptly upon Guilford Lake. On a cold autumn day the water is deep blue among the bare, rounded red and golden hills. This lake is surprisingly large and a real surf beats upon the dam to the east when the wind blows. The western exit of the canal appears at right angles to the road, which obviously required a bridge there in canal days.

From the high dam one sees the firm walls of the canal receding through the meadows eastward, straight toward the deep wooded defile which drops to McKinley Crossing above Lisbon. The formation of the bare hills by the lake creates the impression that it lies in quite a depression; actually, the water must be relatively shallow. We come to the conclusion that this was indeed a flat meadow, for a mile or so east there is the deep-cutting ravine through hills based upon a much lower level. All the earthworks here are strikingly evident, and considerable water lies in the old channels.

One can follow the double green walls of the canal through the wooded cleft and can swing southeast past the old lock stairs to Lisbon, lying deep among the steep hills and ravines of the Middle Beaver, or turn from the eastern end of the lake to cross the south ridge and follow Ohio/U.S. Route 30 westward until the West Fork is crossed by a short but high viaduct. As we approach this we see the canal at the highway level; it is on the western side and shows as a gray shelf on the timbered hillside as it sweeps down and around this ridge toward Dungannon. Here was to have been built the pumping station to feed in the waters of the West Fork. It is evident that the channel, now so high above the creek, still has to pass through the still-rising westward terrain. It therefore continues downstream high above the water until it passes through the first and smaller tunnel northeast of Dungannon.

We continue westward until we strike the road swinging south and east of the latter place, putting us across the ridge of the first tunnel. The canal channel is very evident on the hillside occupied by the village, and one can see it, high-built across the meadow, as it leads from the west end of the first tunnel. This is a peaceful pastoral landscape, rimmed with high hills on all sides.

Retracing our course through the village, we follow the channel but a short distance to see it revealed as a straight water-filled and deeply-shaded ditch disappearing into the shadows of another high hill.

Thus we return to Route 30 and pass this hill on the north. In a matter of minutes Hanoverton appears, and we look back along a wide, deep watery channel to the southeast. This ends abruptly at the ancient rock slide hiding the western end of the Big Tunnel. The mounds of earth and rock which are silhouetted upon the ridge are the material hoisted through the western shaft. The big barn and the few trees on the bare hilltop stand out conspicuously against the sky and are reflected in the stagnant waters on the weedy channel. We see this channel following the highway westward past Hanoverton and into a wider and gentler landscape, foretelling the nearness of the Sandy Valley.

The whole effect of this excursion on a brisk autumn day, with the old works made more visible by the thinning trees, is a tremendous impression of sheer determination unaided by the means of modern construction.

CHAPTER EIGHT

The Pennsylvania Cross-cut

The Pennsylvania and Ohio Canal derived most of its water from the same sources as the Ohio and Erie at the Portage Summit, and flowed eastward until it struck the bend of the Mahoning River on the southern edge of the eastern part of the watershed; it then led down the Mahoning into the Beaver in Pennsylvania. Its popular name, "The Cross-Cut," explains its physical aspects.

In contrast to it, the Sandy–Beaver Canal had to negotiate the foothills of the Alleghenies without adequate feeder ponds. It ran down the Sandy to Bolivar and found a rough course through the mounting foothills to descend rapidly to the Ohio from the neighborhood of Lisbon. It required the building of too many locks to be a paying proposition.

The Cross-Cut connected the Pennsylvania Canal below New Castle with the Ohio and Erie at Akron, a distance of 80 miles. It had feeders from the numerous lakes on the Summit. It was successful for about twelve years from the opening date, 1840, but it was damaged by the coming of the Cleveland and Pittsburgh Railroad through Ravenna in 1851. It is said that the Cleveland and Mahoning Railroad extinguished it. The state sold its canal stock to the second road in 1863. A few boats continued to run after that, picking up what business they could in the more remote sections.

The first letting of contracts for the project took place at New Castle, Pennsylvania on August 10, 1835, when 25 sections, comprising thirteen miles of the eastern division, were let. There were to be in this six locks, eight culverts, one aqueduct over the Shenango; this part was to intersect the Beaver division of the Pennsylvania Canal.

On October 1, 1835, seventeen miles of canal, beginning at McGill's Mill at Poland and extending west to within four miles of Warren, were let, and work was progressing on the Summit. By November 5, sealed proposals were received at Warren for work from Draper's, four miles below Warren to near McClintock's Mill in Newton Falls; also at Ravenna for twenty–seven miles from near McClintock's to section 1 east of the Ravenna Summit; also for section 9 near Franklin Mills (Kent) to the Junction at Akron. There were also six miles of the Cuyahoga Feeder and work on cleaning the reservoirs, together with one or more aqueducts over the Cuyahoga—one across the Mahoning, one over the Little Cuyahoga, and smaller ones over minor streams. There were 25 locks, plus several dams over the Mahoning and many culverts.

On March 1, 1836, bids for 28 bridges, 13 waste weirs, and one culvert were presented to A. Lacock at Youngstown.

A report published on Februry 18, 1839, stated that work on the Cross-Cut had advanced during the winter. There were in the canal 420 feet of lockage. There were four locks, seven culverts, eight bridges, and one aqueduct in Pennsylvania; and 53 locks, one aqueduct, 73 culverts, 57 bridges and nine dams in Ohio. The deep cut on the Summit had been dug to the bottom, and the Little Cuyahoga Feeder was navigable and completed to Middlebury.

May 28, 1839, was the great day at Warren. The "Ontario" arrived with Captain Bronson and forty passengers. They were greeted by a band at the foot of Main Street and marched to Towne's Hotel. An address was delivered to the passengers by John Cromwell, Mayor, and a response was made by B. B. Chamberlain. The opinion of all present was that, "It is the dawn of a new and important era to our town and country."

On June 11, a packet and freight boat was for sale by the builder of the "Ontario," Robert Knox of Pittsburgh. Packet lines were advertising, and steamboats for Pittsburgh could be reached from Warren by the canal.

By May 5, 1840, boats were leaving for both Cleveland and Pittsburgh. The canal was completely navigable, and the Cleveland and Pittsburgh Transportation Company was busy with both freight and passenger traffic. It was announced on May 26 that Lake Erie boats would take passengers to the Fort Meigs celebration at Perrysburg (Miami–Erie Canal) on June 11. Thus began a brief but profitable period in the life of the new canal, which was to last until the expansion of business and the coming of the Cleveland and Pittsburgh Railroad.

As far back as the founding of Cleveland a trail was beaten out Broadway toward Kent, Ravenna, and eastward across the Mahoning headwaters to the Salt Lick at Niles, where the settlers were able to extract much-needed salt from the spring waters there. These licks still exist in part. The trail followed was partly that made by Indians from the mouth of the Beaver to the mouth of Tinkers Creek on the Cuyahoga, and thence by way of Schaaf Road and West 25 Street to Cleveland. This primitive road was also that used to freight flour from Fort Pitt to a depot on West Main Street (Cleveland), destined to be collected and carried by boat to Detroit.

Familiar as this route was, it was not surprising that the people of the Mahoning Valley thought it might be a logical route for a canal. They felt cut off from Lake Erie trade by the watershed west and north, as did the people east of them in Pennsylvania. The Erie Canal was becoming a popular outlet for goods moving to the Atlantic, and Pittsburgh was then an outlet for commerce moving the long way down river to New Orleans.

Anyone studying the map of this region will readily comprehend the advantages to be gained from such a canal when no railroads existed in Ohio. Pittsburgh was an established center; and the Ohio and Erie Canal promised to raise Cleveland in importance, lying as it did between Pittsburgh and Detroit, directly upon a line leading to the mines of the Upper Lakes about to be developed. The people of northeastern Ohio and western Pennsylvania felt this equally, but they did not live upon this vital line of communication, and there was no northward flowing stream of a kind suitable as the companion to a canal.

The people of Erie fought long and bitterly to win prestige in the earlier period, as they tried to join a canal to the southern systems and to block the rail connections eastward and westward. This resentment was like that shown by Sandusky when the Canal Commission abandoned all thought of a Sandusky–Scioto route. Such a route appeared to be enimently reasonable in the light of previous trail and stage travel, but a canal there would have required a much more favorable water supply throughout the year than was available.

The canals and even the railroads adhered closely to the routes followed by the Indian trails; even these last were undoubtedly based upon the migration of buffalo in prehistoric times. Along these routes adequate water would have been found, and such heavy animals avoided steep grades and ridges. The route followed by the Pennsylvania and Ohio Canal was no exception, and today the Pittsburgh and Lake Erie Railroad now traverses the region which was tapped by the canal.

The prospects for the success of the Pennsylvania and Ohio Canal or Cross-Cut were almost as bright as those of the Ohio and Erie. Many Clevelanders were associated with its history, and, for a short time, it did as much as did the first-built canal to enhance the importance of Cleveland. It was only the greater advantage of steam power and rails that forced it into oblivion—that and the fact that its feeder ponds were more or less adjacent to those first tapped by the Ohio and Erie.

Undoubtedly, if modern excavating machinery had been available, the Pennsylvania and Ohio could have been extended northward from the bend of the Mahoning to Fairport, Ashtabula, Conneaut, or Erie, and, through deeper cuts, a waterway would have been made. This was actually contemplated as late as 1904. In that case the towns of Kent and Ravenna would have had a different history, and other towns in Ohio and Pennsylvania would have developed. The present Pymatuning Reservoir was in that day a great shallow marsh; the water impounded there might have filled a deeper ditch for a canal from Pittsburgh to Lake Erie.

To a modern traveller the route followed by the Pennsylvania and Ohio Canal is not remarkable for scenic grandeur, but it is interesting for the evidences of the Great Ice Age recorded there in the form of stony ridges and peat bogs. After leaving the lower basin at Akron by the Goodrich factory, the Pennsylvania and Ohio descended from the Ohio and Erie Cascade by a lock at Mill Street, opposite an important warehouse of the day. It then followed the Little Cuyahoga to Old Forge and passed northeastward, across country marked by ponds and the dark soil created by the glaciers. The descent into the upper loops of the Mahoning is gradual, and there are no deep valleys seen until the lower Mahoning is reached at Warren. From there on the background becomes more impressive, though made harsh today by the presence of industrial plants and railroad yards.

The inhabitants of the valley welcomed the business brought by the canal. Boarding the laborers afforded considerable revenue to the city of Warren during its building. Warehouses were built on the banks, including the principal one on the east side of Main Street which remained standing for many years. The canal entered the town which had a lock into the river at the Van Gorder Dam. This lock was rendered useless at times of high water in the Mahoning.

After reading the records there can be no doubt that the packet travel on this canal was, for a time, more in demand than it was along the Ohio and Erie. Commerce and industry flowed along this line, and raw materials and agricultural products moved upon the other. A system of stationed relay teams was employed to haul the light-built packets, and the towns along the route have a tradition of famous inns and taverns.

The building of the Ohio and Erie and the Pennsylvania and Ohio made the region surrounding Cuyahoga Falls highly important in the minds of people. The scenic beauty of the gorge and the potential water power drew industrialists to the place. Here was a double incentive to creative minds: the junction of two canal lines and a high fall of water.

In studying the topographical maps of Akron we discover that the stone quarry and brook mentioned as supplying lock stone and lime lay below Glendale cemetery and a half mile west of the Little Cuyahoga. This would be in the heart of Akron as we know it, and in the middle of the series of locks forming the Cascade. After the Cross-cut Canal proper diverged at Mill Street, it ran southeast two miles to East Akron or Middlebury, where it crossed the Little Cuyahoga and ascended the shallow valley of a small watercourse toward Tallmadge, then passed northward and down another small watercourse to a point west of Munroe Falls (Wolcott's Mill) and, crossing the main Cuyahoga, led along this river eastward. By this route it passes about a mile and a half east of the Gorge of Cuyahoga Falls, through the western half of Tallmadge Township and strikes the river near the mouth of the "Gulf" southeast of Stow.

The canal then followed the river past Kent (Franklin Mills) and passed up Breakneck Creek (Congress Lake outlet), a mile and a half northeast, near where feeders joined from Lake Pepin and Lake Brady on the north and Muddy and Sandy Lakes on the south. It passed over the summit half a mile southeast of Ravenna, near the line of the Penn Central (Pennsylvania Railroad). About two and a half miles southeast the outlet from Crystal Lake joins the west branch of the Mahoning at Campbellsport, and the cut across the summit was washed through by diverting the water of the outlet of Congress Lake, which lies ten miles or so to the south. Here at the summit the ponds lie at approximately the same level among the hummocky ridges of the glacial moraines. The streams could be turned back by building dikes. The course of the canal was then through Campbellsport at the Bend of the Mahoning eastward and along the north bank. From Newton Falls the course was east northeast.

The canal entered Warren proper at what is now Monumental Park near the Court House. It then followed the east side down toward the Erie and the Baltimore and Ohio Railroads. There was a flax mill where the Western Reserve Bank now stands; and old "hawser rings" were taken out of the wharf here.

The route continued somewhat back from the Mahoning and along the Baltimore and Ohio right of way to the Buckeye Pipe Line and south past the Catholic cemetery above Niles, just below where there was a side-cut into the river. This fact seems to indicate that the river may have been used by barges from thence to Niles and Girard. This immediate region shows definite traces of the old canal, although much of it has been obliterated by industrial plants.

The old Van Gorder Mill at Warren was on the present site of a lumber company office on the northeast side of the river.

Some of the locks of the canal were plainly visible until the flood of 1913, when this washed away what was left. The canal came up to Niles on the north side of the river, cut through Waddell Park at Niles, then left the river and continued on up to Warren at the Buckeye Pipe Line, thence swerving north past the Republic Mill and approaching the river at the Van Gorder Mill.

A view of Youngstown published in Henry Howe's inimitable Ohio records shows the Pennsylvania and Ohio Canal entering that place. This view looks northwest and plainly shows the canal on the left bank of the river, quoted by one authority as being the "right" bank. We may safely assume that this canal kept to the east side of the Mahoning all the way to the Beaver where it joined the Pennsylvania Canal system.

Anyone could use the Pennsylvania and Ohio Canal by paying the required toll, and as many as 25 to 50 boats used to pass through Youngstown daily. The basin lay at Basin Street, where the "canawlers" participated in many knifing affrays with the townsmen. They also fought among themselves and did such things as cutting tow ropes when contesting the right of way.

Use of the canal was profitable for about 25 years, and the last barge, the "Telegraph," carried limestone from Lowellville to Briar Hill in 1872. After this, while the railroads scrambled for the land occupied by the old ditch, the boats rotted where they lay or were used as dwelling shacks by squatters. One such barge was restored and fitted with an engine and a shrill whistle, and was used as an excursion boat between Baldwin's Mill and the Salt Springs Road. This fact proved the Mahoning to be navigable, and a street-railway bought a dam near Mill Creek to prevent competition. The boat people cut a way through this dam and continued operation. In 1895 another steamer was constructed and employed for a similar purpose.

The Pennsylvania and Ohio Canal entered Ohio near the Lowell Gap, the historical route of the Mahoning Valley settlers. The new method of transport brought business to the mills where coal and limestone were used in the making of iron and steel. This almost perennial waterway plan began when rail costs rose, and it was resurrected in 1894 with a new channel projected which was to have a depth of 15 feet, a width of 152 feet and fifty locks. Youngstown men backed this project, which was delayed by the War of 1918. The United States Army made a survey in 1930. There was a setback in 1932 on account of costs; but the idea still lives on in the valley. It was known as the Tri-River Project.

Scenically considered, the Cross-Cut was unique in its first stage at Middlebury, but, until the Mahoning is reached, the landscape is fundamentally commonplace. The height of hills increases as the route approaches Pennsylvania. On the other hand, a fair degree of imagination can invest every mile of this old canal with charm if much of the present-day disfigurement of what must have been a peaceful rural scene is ignored. Even today the reaches between the towns of this industrial region have much beauty about them. The white barges would have lent interest at any season, and their neutral tints would have enhanced the beauty of blossoming orchards or the autumn leaves floating on the still water.

Nevertheless, by 1867 the Pennsylvania and Ohio Canal had outlived its usefulness, and the Legislature authorized the Akron Hydraulic Company to take over the route between the Ravenna Summit and Akron. Later Cuyahoga Falls people resented the presence of the stagnant canal, and some secretly let the water "percolate" out. There was a sale of canal property to the Mahoning Railroad, and in 1874 South Main Street (Akron) people turned the water into the Ohio Canal and into the lowlands about. The land reverted in part to the original owners.

Today, as a southbound train slides out of Ravenna, we find ourselves emerging from low hillocks, and suddenly the twin banks of the Pennsylvania and Ohio Canal parallel the track and then swing into second-growth timber to the left and north. The ground drops away immediately toward the Mahoning; we see the channel once or twice as it bears off northward.

We soon pass the long stretch of buildings making up the Ravenna Arsenal, meanwhile becoming aware of a highway lying between this and the railroad. The fact that this highway lies within, and sometimes on either side of, the canal is not apparent at first; but near Newton Falls, the channel lies practically untouched across the meadows of the angle between the branch and the main stream of the Mahoning River.

The steel industry has obliterated all signs of the canal along the Mahoning. Apparently these railroads utilized the well-planned grade of the old canal; the bridges stand most probably where the old guardlock lay. But little of the channel down the left bank can be seen except occasional short sections in the older parts of Girard, Niles, and Youngstown, which have not been used as furnace or factory sites. These spots bear a strong resemblance to the lower portions of the Cascade Race at Akron, and a sharp and discerning eye is required to locate them.

The tortuous and irregular pattern of the hummocks on the Ravenna Summit is further complicated by railroad embankments, buildings and street grading, so that it would require considerable study to follow the precise route on foot. But one will not be disappointed by what may be found in the neighborhood of Newton Falls. This place has preserved everything which suggests older days.

When one has followed the various canal routes with a view to the physical difficulties involved in their construction, he may well come to the conclusion that the Pennsylvania and Ohio route was quite the most feasible of all. The mere fact that the summit was so plentifully supplied with water is significant, and also that this water was made to do much of the work in forming the deep cut there. There are, all along the way, wide meadows between the channel and the foothills. At least there were no such cut banks as were found along the Cuyahoga and other streams. The Mahoning is not a rapid river, and it is fed by numerous streams carrying a strong head of water.

The Mahoning cuts its way through the Ohio Plateau as far as Youngstown but does not reveal its presence from a distance. The back country is generally flat or rolling, but the banks beyond the flood-plain are high and impressive. Formerly the white barges glided by slowly under the eastern sides, where now many furnaces smoke and slag dumps have covered the channel. Below Youngstown the hills rise higher as the river winds through the Uplift of the Alleghenies. Before the days of the steel industry, this must have been a picturesque portion of the route. In view of the great changes in this section of the state, we may take a certain satisfaction from the fact that the canal played an important part in the development of the region.

CHAPTER NINE

The Passing
of the Canals

The canals of Ohio alone extended for about a thousand miles throughout the state, and they cost $16 million in the relatively greater money value of those days. Their importance as a means of transportation declined after 1860, and they ceased to function in a practical way around 1900. The state restored some of the sections a few years later, ostensibly for the use of pleasure craft; but after that they fell into complete decay. Small portions of these waterways remain in service as feeders for the water supply of industrial plants.

When it became evident in 1861 that the usefulness of the canals was passing, portions of the system were leased by the state to a company for ten years. This contract was renewed for ten years more; but such property reverted to the state in 1879. As early as 1872 three miles of the canal terminal were given to the City of Cincinnati on April 27, to be used by the railroads.

Even if it was later found to be more profitable to use railroads for the transportation of freight, the early tolls on the Miami and Erie Canal are said to have been relatively low, e.g., the toll on a barrel of salt carried from Cleveland to Portsmouth on the Ohio and Erie was 21 cents for 309 miles, and that to Nelsonville on the Hocking Canal, 152 miles, was 26 cents. The passenger fare on the Miami and Erie was five cents per passenger mile. Rates on long and short hauls began to cause difficulty in 1850, probably owing to competition with the railroads.

One of the disadvantages of many canals afflicted the Miami and Erie, since this canal lost seven weeks a year

The Coming Change in Transport — Cleveland.

because of freeze-ups. The state continued its policy of abandonment in 1876 with part of the Hocking, and in 1888 all of the Wabash and Erie was done away with. The Walhonding was practically abandoned in 1896, and in 1906 only the Ohio and Erie and the Miami and Erie were in operation and only partially so at that. The state derived revenue from these waterways by leasing water power rights to private companies at this time.

Among the various projects for the use of the Miami and Erie Channel was a Ship Canal plan of 1879–80.

With the abandonment of the old waterways and the lack of supervision of the property, there was much spoliation of such property. In 1888 much lock stone was appropriated along with other property at Toledo. The railroads and other interests disputed their rights to abandoned canal property, and it was found that many parties held unauthorized leases on land acquired in good faith. Many former water power mills on the banks of canals had, by this time, turned to the use of steam, but they were reluctant to resign their locations. The question arose as to the meaning of the term "canal bed"; did this include the towpath and the berme bank or the basin only? It was proved on investigation that much property was occupied for which no record of title could be found.

Even before the canal days were over, the bicycle became popular and people found that the towpath made an ideal road to the country. This was before the true lanes or roads were passable to anything but horse-drawn vehicles. Our local roads were clay and treacherous when wet, and the towpath was no exception. Many a Clevelander has been known to skid into the canal to the merriment of spectators—canal boatmen, fishermen and co-cyclists. However, the towpath made it possible to ride great distances through a sylvan landscape which the modern highway misses completely. All down the canal were places of intense interest that have changed, such as the Zoar of the older days. This place was once a Mecca for Cleveland artists who rode down there on their "wheels."

About 1907 contracts were let by the state to companies interested in the new art of pouring concrete for the purpose of reconstructing some of the locks and sluices of the Miami and Erie and the Ohio and Erie. This was ostensibly to make these canals serviceable for pleasure boating above Cleveland and Toledo; also, presumably to perpetuate available water power for the use of industrial plants in those cities. The old Ohio Canal still serves this purpose in south Cleveland. Actually, the older stonework has outlasted the restoration in a few places, and the pleasure parties anticipated failed to come up to expectations. Toledo people used the Lower Miami to a degree, but no true canal barge ever passed through the new locks.

If one seeks to trace the courses of the Ohio canals today, he will discover that, besides the portions remaining intact, many miles of the waterways have been converted into boulevards and highways, while others have been built over in other ways or have been merely leveled and plowed under. Portions which have been fortunately preserved remain near Cleveland, Akron, Massillon, Coshocton, and Roscoe on the

95

Ohio–Erie, and between Texas and Defiance on the Miami–Erie. The great reservoirs of Indian Lake, Buckeye Lake, Lake St. Marys, and the various ponds at Akron, south and east, preserve the memory of the canals. Even Guilford Lake has proved more permanent than the Sandy–Beaver Canal.

Also, in a sense, the conservation dams, recently constructed, lie upon many of the canal sites. We see these at Zoar, in the Walhonding and its headwaters, above Dover, and along the Muskingum. Some of the long feeders adjacent to these lakes will probably remain for a considerable time to remind the student of history that the canals were once important to the people of Ohio.

The lower Scioto River and the lower Miami River have been permanently marked by the use of protective embankments which have been included in and extended by water control projects. There can be little doubt that the knowledge gained through the building and use of canals has been of great value in later days, when deforestation has resulted in disastrous floods and great loss of property and life. When the canals were first built, we know that the general forestation acted as a sponge of immense proportions to absorb storm water or the melting of winter snows; but in recent years we have had to restrain suddenly-gathered waters which have flowed down the channels of the former canals or the headwaters leading to them.

The continual fight put up by the operators of the canals to curb this excess of water seemed never-ending; this was because the condition was constantly increasing with the years. Farmers continued to plow without regard for the

96

preservation of the topsoil; and this was washed into the canals as well as into the rivers. The lack of power dredges always necessitated the drawing off of the water in a section or level until the clearing could be accomplished, and the increasing cost lessened the ability of the canal operators to cope with it.

If the railroads, or even the traction lines, had not been commercial rivals, it is quite possible that means would have been found to mend the situation in time to save the canals.

This does not necessarily mean that the canals might not have been modified in their operation, their depth, or their courses. They might still connect lakes and slack-water reaches of our rivers if they had not been completely neglected. The later work on our conservation projects shows that, if they had been fondly regarded, they could have been preserved by modern engineering methods. Nor does this mean that their slight value to transport might not have been offset by their usefulness in a continuous State Park System which might have paid dividends in another way.

It would be only natural that anyone reading of the old canals might ask where and to what degree visual evidences of the system exist. Such evidences range from locks and sections of embankment quite intact to portions completely obliterated by modern grading. The greater part of the old lines however can be found in that half-seen state which piques the imagination and provokes curiosity and questioning. Such matters include the weathered banks, sunken and despoiled locks, old buildings still showing adaptations to the handling of canal freight and patterns of roads and streets which were determined by these former watercourses.

At the present writing the best place to study the Ohio and Erie Canal is between the Willow Cloverleaf south of Cleveland, and the Brecksville Dam which provides the water for the American Steel & Wire Company at Harvard Avenue in Cleveland. A ride out Canal Road will afford opportunity to see three locks complete, sluices, an aqueduct at Tinkers Creek, and also the Brecksville feeder. Sad to say, no barges can now be seen in any of the old canals.

The Akron district affords evidence of a sort to whet the explorer's interest, while Lock No. 1 and the dry-dock are quite intact. The system of lakes and channels south of the city is revealing to any interested person. The neighborhood of Massillon preserves sylvan vistas of the old channel and a sharp eye traces the canal through the town through the study of architectural details.

The long descent of the canal toward Coshocton is marked by the Zoar Lock and interrupted sections above Dover; and the river highway gives glimpses of old widewaters in the prairies just above Coshocton. A lock at Roscoe, quite hidden by second growth, exists to tempt one to explore the section of canal leading up the Walhonding toward the modern conservation dam.

After ascending the Licking and attaining the summit south of Newark one may see stone ramparts marking old lock sites, and, at Buckeye Lake, the outlet has been preserved. In the flatter sections of the southern portion of the Ohio and Erie Canal agriculture has quite obliterated much of the route. It is in the matter of architecture, such as mills and warehouses, that one finds much to study at New Washington and other villages along the system. At the latter place an old warehouse straddles the canal where barges were loaded through the floor of the building. Throughout the system the hooded pulley-shaft in the peak of the gable is the tell-tale sign of the former canal traffic.

Only an engineer or archeologist could properly trace the Pennsylvania Cross-Cut—one with a true eye for topography; but the Sandy–Beaver, although difficult of access in many places, affords the most romantic satisfaction. The Guilford Reservoirs on the highlands west of Lisbon are beautiful and, although the westward channel is empty, the course can be traced through the two hills and down the Sandy. The wild eerie eastern approach to the Big Tunnel may be viewed by risking brambles and a precarious footing in the rubble of the excavation.

The abortive project of the canal from Canton to the Sandy shows slight evidence, and the Columbus Feeder and other like stretches of canal have, in many places, been obliterated by roadfills. The Hocking Canal, so early abandoned, would be intrinsically more interesting than others, for it passed through what remains of a beautiful and romantic landscape.

Perhaps the most satisfactory of all the canals to study at the present time is the Maumee section of the Miami and Erie Canal. One leaves Toledo on the Anthony Wayne Trail, which is a canal fill, and finds the Side-Cut Park at Maumee where the great locks appear as picturesque ruins in a park made to preserve them. Another feature is the guardlock, slip and turning basin at Grand Rapids; and both here and

97

at Waterville are old buildings. The guardlock and channel below Texas appear beside the river highway which in part occupies the channel. Further west the canal is being preserved at Independence and the locks restored.

It is unfortunate that so little has been preserved at Defiance where once existed the famous towing bridge and the wooden locks of the Auglaize Section. Old embankments appear occasionally as one drives south toward the St. Marys Summit; and the Wabash and Erie, westward from Junction, might well be mistaken for a large drainage ditch in the flat ploughed fields.

The many efforts made since thecanal days to control the floodwaters of the Miami and its tributary, the Mad River, have created earthworks and dikes enough to confuse the eye of the explorer from Piqua down. Indian Lake outlet was a navigable feeder leading toward that of the Loramie Reservoir just above the city. No doubt a little study might provide more than can be mentioned here regarding the Lebanon Canal and other parts of the system.

Strangely enough, evidences persist longest where it was most difficult to dig ditches and create fills originally. The high banks and works along the Maumee are the best preserved of abandoned sections; and evidences are usually clear in narrow defiles where modern agriculture has not obliterated old channels, and modern building is impractical. One should appreciate the fact that modern engineering facilities can ignore most of the impediments of nature; while man, in building the canals, preserved to his advantage the original character of the topography as much as possible in order to avail himself of the gravitational flow of the precious water upon which canal barges floated. Thus several interests animate the canal hunter—his interests in the works of man and the degree to which nature assisted or worked against him in her determination to preserve her own.

The maintenance of the right of way was a spring and summer problem on the canals. If the rigors of spring frost had their effect on banks and locks, summer brought a heavy growth of plants both on the banks and in the water. This required much supervision by the state. As the freight barges were privately owned, tolls paid for such work as was needed. This system apparently made it difficult to keep up the waterway during periods of depression.

Bibliography

I. GENERAL WORKS

Campbell, William W. *Life and Writings of DeWitt Clinton*. New York: Bates and Scribner, 1849.

Cherry, P. P. *The Portage Path*. Akron, Ohio: Western Reserve Co., 1911.

Crouse, D. E. *The Ohio Gateway*. New York: Charles Schribner's Sons, 1931.

Crow, George H. and Smith, C. P. *My State Ohio*. Columbus, Ohio: Ohio Teacher Pub. Co., 1931.

Dictionary of American History. New York: Charles Scribner's Sons, 1940.

History of the Hocking Valley, Ohio. Chicago: Inter-State Pub. Co., 1883.

History of the Lower Scioto Valley, Ohio. Chicago: Inter-State Pub. Co., 1884.

History of the Maumee Valley. Toledo: H. S. Knapp, 1887.

History of the Upper Ohio Valley. Madison, Wisconsin: Brant and Fuller, 1891.

Hopkins, Charles Edwin. *Ohio the Beautiful and Historic*. Boston: L. C. Page & Co., 1931.

Hover, John C. and Barnes, Joseph D., editors. *Memoirs of the Miami Valley*. Chicago: Robt. O. Law Co., 1919.

Howe, Henry. *Historical Collections of Ohio*. Norwalk, Ohio: State of Ohio, by Laning Printing Co., 1896.

Lewis, Thomas William. *History of Southeastern Ohio and the Muskingum Valley*. Chicago: S. J. Clarke Pub. Co., 1928.

The Ohio Guide. Compiled by workers of the Writer's Program of the Work Projects Administration in the State of Ohio. New York: Oxford University Press, 1940.

State Centennial History of Ohio. Madison, Wisconsin: Northwestern Historical Association, 1902.

Thomas, B. F. and Watts, D. A. *The Muskingum River, Ohio*. New York: J. Wiley & Sons, 1903.

II. CANALS

Bishop, Martin. *Canal Locks. Zanesville Advocate*, 1872.

Board of Canal Commissioners of the State of Ohio: Annual Reports. Columbus.

Bortel, Clifford R. *Old Canal Days at Texas, Ohio*. Northwestern Ohio Historical Quarterly, April, 1947.

Davis, Harold E. *Pennsylvania and Ohio Canal*. Hiram Historical Association, *Garrettsville Journal*, 1929.

Delaware and Raritan Canal. Annual Report, 1831.

Galbraith, G. B. *The Ohio Canal*. Springfield, Ohio: Springfield Pub. Co., 1910.

George, John J., Jr. *The Miami Canal*. Columbus: *Ohio Archeological and Historical Quarterly*, 1927.

Gilmore, W. *Over Ohio Hills in a Canal Boat*. Canton, Ohio: 1935.

History of Ohio Canal. Ohio State Archeological and Historical Society. Columbus: F. J. Heer, 1905.

Hulburt, Archer Butler. *The Great American Canals*. Cleveland: A. H. Clark Co., 1904.

Kilbourn, John. *Public Document Concerning Ohio Canals*. Columbus: 1828–1832.

Laws Relating to State Lands. Ohio Canal Commission. Columbus.

Memorial on the Hocking Canal. Shawnee, Hocking Valley and Columbus Railroad Co. Columbus, 1879.

Pennsylvania and Ohio Canal. Charter. Columbus: 1837.

Portage Canal and Manufacturing Co. Charter. New York: Piekey and Reed, 1837.

Porter, Burton P. *Old Canal Days*. Columbus: Heer Printing Co., 1942.

Rules, Specifications—Hocking Valley Canal Co. Athens, Ohio: A. Vorhes, Printer, 1837.

Rules and Specifications for Construction of Ohio Canals. Columbus: S. Medary, 1843.

Travis, Irven. *The Muskingum River Improvement—The McConnelsville Lock Old and New*. Columbus: *Ohio Archeological and Historical Quarterly*, 1910.

White, George Dial. *Construction of the Ohio Canals*. Columbus: *Ohio Archeological and Historical Quarterly*.

III. CITIES

AKRON

Atlas of Akron, Ohio. Akron, Ohio, 1891.

Centennial History of Akron, 1825–1925. Akron, Beacon Journal Co., 1925.

Kanfield, Scott Dix, ed. *Akron and Summit County, Ohio*. Chicago, Akron: S. J. Clarke Pub. Co., 1928.

Lane, Samuel A. *Fifty Years and Over of Akron and Summit County*. Akron, Beacon Job Dept., 1892.

Olin, Oscar Eugene. *Akron and Environs—Historical Biographical and Genealogical*. Chicago and New York: Lewis Pub Co., 1917.

CINCINNATI

Cincinnati, A Guide to the Queen City and its Neighbors. Compiled by the workers of the Writer's Program of the Work Projects Administration in the State of Ohio. Cincinnati: Wieser-Hart Press, 1943.

History of Cincinnati and Hamilton County, Ohio. Cincinnati: S. B. Nelson & Co., 1894.

Roe, George Mortimer, editor. *Cincinnati, the Queen City of the West*. Cincinnati: C. J. Krehbiel Co., 1895.

CLEVELAND

Annals of Cleveland, 1818–1925. Multigraphed by Cleveland Works Project Administration, 1936, Project No. 14066.

Benton, Elbert Jay. *Cultural Story of an American City: Cleveland*. Cleveland: Western Reserve Society, 1943.

COLUMBUS

Taylor, William Alexander. *Centennial History of Columbus and Franklin County*. Columbus: S. J. Clarke Pub. Co., 1909.

DAYTON

Conover, Charlotte Reeve, editor. *Dayton and Montgomery County, Ohio—Resources and People.* New York: Lewis Historical Pub. Co., 1932.

HAMILTON

Heiser, Alta Harvey. *Hamilton in the Making.* Oxford, Ohio: Mississippi Valley Press, 1941.

NEWARK

Brister, E. M. P. *Centennial History of Newark and Licking County, Ohio.* Chicago and Columbus: S. J. Clarke Pub Co., 1909.

TOLEDO

History of the City of Toledo and Lucas County, Ohio. New York and Toledo: Munsell and Co., 1888.

Killits, John M., editor. *Toledo and Lucas County, Ohio.* Chicago and Toledo: S. J. Clarke Pub. Co., 1923.

Scribner, Harvey S. *Memoirs of Lucas County and the City of Toledo.* Madison, Wisconsin: Western Historical Association, 1916.

TROY

Harbaugh, Thomas C. *Troy, Piqua and Miami County, Ohio.* Chicago: Richmond-Arnold Pub. Co., 1909.

YOUNGSTOWN

Butler, Joseph G., Jr. *History of Youngstown and the Mahoning Valley, Ohio.* Chicago and New York: American Historical Society, 1921.

IV. COUNTIES

ALLEN

Rusler, William. *History of Allen County, Ohio.* Chicago and New York: American Historical Society, 1921.

ATHENS

Atlas of Athens County, Ohio. Philadelphia: Titus, Simmons and Titus, 1875.

Martzolff, Clement L. *Brief History of Athens County, Ohio.* Athens, Ohio, pub. by Author, 1916.

Walker, Charles M. *History of Athens County, Ohio.* Cincinnati: Robt. Clarke & Co., 1869.

AUGLAIZE

McMurray, William James. *History of Auglaize County, Ohio.* Indianapolis: Historical Pub. Co., 1923.

Simkins, Joshua Dean. Auglaize County, Ohio. St. Marys, Ohio: Argus Printing Co., 1901.

BUTLER

Centennial History of Butler County, Ohio. B. F. Bowen & Co., 1905.

CARROLL

Eckley, W. J. and Perry, William T., editors. *History of Carroll and Harrison County, Ohio.* New York: Lewis Pub. Co., 1921.

Illustrated Historical Atlas of Carroll County, Ohio. Chicago: H. H. Hardesty Co., 1874.

COLUMBIANA

Atlas of Columbiana County, Ohio. Philadelphia: C. C. Titus, 1870.

Atlas of Columbiana County, Ohio. Lisbon, Ohio: Columbiana Map and Atlas Co., 1902.

Barth, Harold B. *History of Columbiana County, Ohio.* Topeka-Indianapolis: Historical Pub. Co., 1926.

COSHOCTON

Hill, N. N., Jr. *History of Coshocton County, Ohio.* Newark, Ohio: A. A. Graham & Co., 1881.

Hunt, William E. *Historical Collections of Coshocton County, Ohio.* Cincinnati: Robt. Clarke & Co., 1876.

CUYAHOGA

Johnson, Crisfield. *History of Cuyahoga County, Ohio.* Cleveland: D. W. Ensign and Co., 1879.

Lake, D. J. *Atlas of Cuyahoga County, Ohio.* Philadelphia: Titus, Simmons and Titus, 1874.

DEFIANCE

Hardesty, Hiram H. *Atlas of Defiance County and Fulton County, Ohio.* Chicago: H. H. Hardesty & Co., 1875.

ERIE

Aldrich, Lewis Cass. *History of Erie County, Ohio.* Syracuse, New York: D. Mason and Co., 1889.

Combination Atlas Map of Erie County, Ohio. Philadelphia: Stewart and Page, 1874.

Peeke, H. L. *Centennial History of Erie County, Ohio.* Cleveland: Penton Press, 1925.

Peeke, Hewson L. *History of Erie County, Ohio.* New York: Lewis Pub. Co., 1916.

FAIRFIELD

Hannum's Atlas of Fairfield County, Ohio. Lancaster, Ohio: E. S. Hannum, 1866.

Scott, Hervey. *Complete History of Fairfield County, Ohio.* Columbus: Siebert and Lilley, 1877.

FRANKLIN

History of Franklin and Pickaway County. Cleveland: Williams Bros., 1880.

Taylor, William Alexander. *Centennial History of Columbus and Franklin County.* Columbus, Ohio: S. J. Clarke Pub. Co., 1909.

FULTON

Aldrich, Lewis Cass. *History of Henry and Fulton County, Ohio.* Syracuse, N. Y.: D. Mason & Co., 1888.

Hardesty, Hiram H. *Atlas of Defiance County and Fulton County, Ohio.* Chicago H. H. Hardesty & Co., 1875.

HAMILTON

Ford, H. A. and Ford, K. B. *History of Hamilton County, Ohio.* Cleveland: L. A. Williams & Co., 1881.

Harrison, R. R., et al. *Atlas of Hamilton County, Ohio.* Philadelphia: C. O. Titus, 1864.

History of Cincinnati and Hamilton County, Ohio. Cincinnati: S. B. Nelson & Co., 1894.

Teetor, Henry B. *The Past and Present of Mill Creek Valley.* Cincinnati: Cohen & Co., 1882.

HARRISON

Eckley, W. J. and Perry, William T., Editors. *History of Carroll and Harrison County, Ohio.* Chicago and New York: Lewis Pub. Co., 1921.

104

HENRY

Aldrich, Lewis Cass. *History of Henry and Fulton County.* Syracuse, N. Y.: D. Mason & Co., 1888.

HOCKING

Atlas of Hocking County. Philadelphia: Titus, Simmons and Titus, 1876.

LICKING

Beers, Frederick W. *Atlas of Licking County, Ohio.* New York: Beers, Soule and Co., 1866.

Brister, E. M. P. *Centennial History of Newark and Licking County, Ohio.* Chicago and Columbus: S. J. Clarke Pub. Co., 1909.

Hill, N. N., Jr. *History of Licking County, Ohio.* Newark, Ohio: A. A. Graham & Co., 1881.

McKinley, John D. *The Black Hand.* Columbus: Archeological and Historical Quarterly, 1904.

Smucker, Isaac. *Centennial History of Licking County, Ohio.* Newark, Ohio: Clark and Underwood, 1876.

LUCAS

Hardesty, Hiram H. *Atlas of Lucas County, Ohio.* Chicago and Toledo: H. H. Hardesty and Co., 1882.

History and Atlas of Lucas County, Ohio. Toledo, Ohio: The Uhl Bros. Co., 1901.

History of the City of Toledo and Lucas County, Ohio. New York and Toledo: Munsell and Co., 1888.

Killits, John M., editor. *Toledo and Lucas County, Ohio.* Chicago and Toledo: S. J. Clarke Co., 1923.

Scribner, Harvey S. *Memoirs of Lucas County and the City of Toledo.* Madison, Wisconsin: Western Historical Association, 1916.

MAHONING

Lake, D. J. *Atlas of Mahoning County, Ohio.* Philadelphia: Titus, Simmons and Titus, 1874.

MIAMI

Harbaugh, Thomas C. *Troy, Piqua and Miami County, Ohio.* Chicago: Richmond-Arnold Pub. Co., 1909.

History of Miami County, Ohio. Chicago: W. H. Beers Co., 1880.

MONTGOMERY

Conover, Charlotte Reeve, editor. *Dayton and Montgomery County, Ohio— Resources and People.* New York: Lewis Historical Pub. Co., 1932.

Everts, L. H. *New Historical Atlas of Montgomery County, Ohio.* Philadelphia: Hunter, Printer, 1875.

MUSKINGUM

Atlas of Muskingum County, Ohio. New York: Beers Soule & Co., 1866.

PICKAWAY

History of Franklin and Pickaway County. Cleveland, Ohio: Williams Bros., 1880.

Van Cleaf, Aaron R. *History of Pickaway County, Ohio.* Chicago: Biographical Pub. Co., 1906.

PORTAGE

Atlas of Portage County, Ohio. Cleveland: H. B. Stranahan & Co., 1900.

History of Portage County, Ohio. Chicago: Warner, Beers & Co., 1885.

New Historical Atlas of Portage County, Ohio. Chicago: L. H. Everts, 1874.

SCIOTO

Evans, Nelson W. *History of Scioto County.* Portsmouth, Ohio: N. W. Evans, 1903.

SHELBY

Atlas of Shelby County, Ohio. Philadelphia: Page and Smith, 1875.

Hitchcock, A. B. C. *History of Shelby County, Ohio.* Chicago: Richmond-Arnold Pub. Co., 1913.

STARK

Atlas of Stark County, Ohio. New York: F. W. Beers and Co., 1870.

Blue, Herbert T. O. *History of Stark County, Ohio.* Chicago: S. J. Clarke Clarke Pub. Co., 1928.

SUMMIT

Atlas of Summit County, Ohio, Philadelphia: Tackaberry, Mead and Moffett, 1874.

Atlas of Summit County, Ohio. Akron Map and Atlas Company, 1891.

Kenfield, Scott Dix, editor. *Akron and Summit County, Ohio.* Chicago, Akron: S. J. Clarke Pub. Co., 1928.

Lane, Samuel A. *Fifty Years and Over of Akron and Summit County.* Akron, Beacon Job Dept., 1892.

TRUMBULL

Atlas of Trumbull County, Ohio. Cleveland: American Atlas Co., 1899.

Everts, L. H. *New Historical Atlas of Trumbull County, Ohio.* Chicago: L. H. Everts, 1874.

TUSCARAWAS

First Centennial History and Atlas of Tuscarawas County. New Philadelphia, Ohio: Edwin S. Rhodes, 1908.

History of Tuscarawas County. Chicago: Warner, Beers & Co., 1884.

Lorman, H. P. *History of Early Tuscarawas County, Ohio.* Tuscarawas County Historical Society: Acme Printing Co., 1930.

Richardson, J. M. *Brief History of Tuscarawas County, Ohio.* Canal Dover, Ohio: Bixler Printing Co., 1896.

WARREN

Everts, L. H. *Atlas Map of Warren County, Ohio.* Philadelphia: Hunter Press, 1875.